24

JESUS' FINAL HOURS

AN HOUR-BY-HOUR BREAKDOWN OF JESUS' FINAL 24 HOURS

THE CHRONOLOGY OF JESUS' LIFE – PART 2

JOHN MAXWELL

24

JESUS' FINAL HOURS

Twenty-four hours – one turn of the Earth on its axis

Most days blend into each other, but one day changed the world forever:

The day Jesus Christ, the Son of God died

The following events took place from 18:20 Hours on Thursday to 18:20 Hours on Friday on the Eve of the Feast of Passover in Jerusalem.

Special thanks

All glory and honour to God! With special thanks to my beautiful wife, Yeng, my father and mother, John and Eileen, the Chuah family, Charles Harbottle, Austin McDermott and David Goodship for all their love, help, support and prayers.

24 – JESUS' FINAL HOURS

ISBN-9798373378284

Published 2023

Edited by Yeng Maxwell

Scripture quotations are based on the World English Bible (WEB) which is in the public domain. The WEB is a 1997 version of the American Standard Version of 1901.

Contents

Introduction

Whether you would like to admit it or not, the most important event in world history is the death of Jesus Christ, the Son of God on the cross of Calvary.

All events in history prior to Jesus' crucifixion led to that point and all events since have led from that point. As I wrote Part One of the Jesus Chronology series, '*The Jesus Diary*'[1], the most complete chronology of his life ever written, the events of the Crucifixion affected me deeply. Seeing what he suffered to free me and mankind from sin has inspired me to look at events in his final hours in more detail. Believing what is written in the Bible made it possible to break down events of his final day into twenty-four, one-hour sections. Examining the chronology of the most timeless event in history that was conceived before time began and the consequences of which will last forever, reveals so much of God's heart and His selfless love and nature. 'Jesus' Final Hours' – Part Two of the Jesus Chronology series shows the suffering God's Son endured to set us free from our sins and reveals the love behind his selfless sacrifice. It shows the part each person played in his Passion and the effect those events had on them and has on us.

If the Gospels dedicate so much content to Jesus' final hours, then we should give them our full attention. This book focuses on the main events around the Crucifixion. Read the Scriptures for each event. Hear what God is saying to you in that event. As you read the passage and a verse stands out, it will be the one God is drawing to your attention. Meditate and pray on that verse. Ask God what He is saying to you in His word and receive a new revelation of Jesus our Saviour, who is fully God and fully man. Then watch your faith grow.

First, let's look at the method needed to establish a timeframe for the events of Jesus' final twenty-four hours on planet Earth:

Methodology

To break events of Jesus' last day into a twenty-four hour timeframe, we need to believe what is written in the Bible. It is the method used to write, 'The Jesus Diary'[1] and it produced the fullest chronology of events in his life ever written. It will do the same for this hour-by-hour record of Jesus' last day, which began when he arrived at the house for the Last Supper as evening came (Mark 14:17). Evenings begin at sunset. In the current year the Jerusalem solar calendar says the sun sets on the day before Passover at 18:20 Hours[a]. The time it sets has not changed over the years. If it sets at that time today it would have set at that time on the day before Jesus died. The final event that day was his burial, which occurred as the Sabbath was about to begin (Luke 23:53-54). Sabbaths begin at sunset. The sun set that Friday at 18:20 Hours. It means events in Jesus' final twenty-four hours began at 18:20 Hours on Thursday and ended at 18:20 Hours on Friday.

There is a midpoint to events in Jesus' final hours. Luke 22:66 says the Jewish leaders condemned Jesus at daybreak. Daybreak is dawn. The Jerusalem solar calendar says dawn breaks at Passover in the current year at 05:50 Hours[a]. As the time dawn breaks has not changed over time, it would have broken at 05:50 Hours on the day Jesus died. That would mean all of the events prior to him being condemned to die by the religious leaders would have happened from 18:20 Hours on Thursday to 05:50 Hours on Friday. And all of the events after Jesus was condemned by the religious leaders would have taken place from 05:50 Hours to 18:20 Hours on Friday.

Events in this book are recorded in hour-by-hour sections. As you join me on this moment-by-moment journey of Jesus' final hours you will discover more of the character and love of our Lord and Saviour, who died for our sins and the sins of the world on the cross of Calvary. First, let's examine historical records outside the Gospels to show Jesus Christ, the Son of God existed in human history.

Jesus in historical records

The Gospels say Jesus was killed by Pilate, governor of Judea in the reign of Roman Emperor Tiberius. Historical evidence for events in Tiberius' reign is scarce. Four historians wrote of his reign and two mentioned Jesus – Tacitus mentioned him directly and Suetonius indirectly. This is not the Bible or Christian writing, but historical texts of the events of Tiberius' reign. It is surprising any historian should mention Jesus. He was a Jewish preacher crucified in a far flung part of the Empire – Israel, which was of no interest to those in Rome. They did not write about him because they were interested in him. They wrote about him because the Empire was filled with Christians and it was a problem for their leaders. When their historians looked at where they came from, they traced it back to one man, Jesus of Nazareth, who was crucified by Pilate. Christians came from Jesus.

Tacitus

Tacitus wrote about events in Emperor Nero's reign. In May 64AD Rome caught fire and it destroyed ten of Rome's fourteen provinces. Rumour spread Nero had caused the fire. He had talked of knocking down the city and rebuilding it to his design. To quell the rumours, he blamed the fire on the Christians, saying there were so many of them and they said there would be a day of judgment by fire when the world would end. Nero said Christians started the fire in Rome in order to bring about the end of the world by fire. Tacitus wrote the following:

'Nero fastened the guilt on a class hated for their abominations called Christians. Christus from whom the name originated, suffered the extreme penalty during Tiberius' reign at the hands of Pilate, a most mischievous superstition, thus checked for the moment broke out not only in Judea, the source of the evil but even in Rome.'[2]

Tacitus' unsympathetic reference to Jesus and early Christians tells us their name came from the historical person – Christ, who suffered the extreme penalty (crucifixion) under Pilate during Tiberius' reign.

Suetonius

Roman historian, Suetonius wrote about Jesus because the number of Christians in the Empire was a problem. He wrote a history of the Emperors of Rome, called 'The Lives of the Caesars'[3], in which Suetonius recorded this event during the reign of Emperor Claudius:

'The Jews were constantly making disturbances at the instigation of Christus (his term for Christ). And because of this man Christ there was so much trouble Claudius expelled all the Jews from Rome.'[4]

It is a well-established historical fact that in 43AD, Claudius drove all Jews out of Rome, because they were having big fights and quarrels over this man called Jesus, and the writings of Roman historian, Suetonius confirm this. The historical accounts say Christians filled the Empire. When writers investigated where they came from they found Pilate crucified Jesus in Tiberius' reign from the records kept in Rome, which Pilate had sent back from Israel. From them the source of where it all came from was traced back to Jesus of Nazareth.

Josephus

Jewish historian, Josephus also wrote about Jesus. The text may have been corrupted in later translations, but it does not diminish proof of Josephus' writing confirming Jesus' existence. He wrote:

'Now there was about this time, Jesus, a wise man, if it be lawful to call him a man, for he was a doer of wonderful works – a teacher of such men as receive the truth with pleasure. He drew over to him both many of the Jews and many of the Gentiles. He was Christ; and when Pilate, at the suggestion of the principal men amongst us had condemned him to the cross, those that loved him at first did not forsake him, for he appeared to them alive again the third day, as the divine prophets had foretold these and ten thousand other wonderful things concerning him; and the tribe of Christians so named after him, are not extinct to date.'[5]

Gospel reliability

There is proof of Jesus' existence in historical records outside the Bible. If the Gospels are to be used to establish a chronology of final hour events, it is vital to prove the reliability of their content. Some may say they were written so long ago they are not reliable. We know the text has not changed over time from the science of textural criticism. It says the more texts there are and the closer they were written to the event, the less doubt there is about the authenticity of the original text. In his book, *'Are the New Testament Documents Reliable?'*[6] FF Bruce shows how rich the New Testament is in text attestation by comparing it to other historical works.

He shows ten copies of Caesar's Gallic War exist. The oldest text was written nine hundred years after Caesar's day. Twenty copies of Livy's Roman History exist. The earliest text was written nine hundred years after events. Twenty copies of the fourteen books of the Histories of Tacitus survive. Of the sixteen books of his Annals ten parts of his works rely on two manuscripts, written nine hundred and a thousand years after events. The History of Thucydides relies on eight texts written around 900AD, thirteen hundred years after events occurred. There are eight copies of the History of Herodotus, written thirteen hundred years after events. However, no classical scholar doubts the authenticity of these works despite their rarity and the large time gaps between events and their recordings. The New Testament was written from 40AD to 100AD. There are full texts dating from 350AD (just 300 years after events) and papyri with most of the New Testament texts dating from the third century. A fragment of John's Gospel dates from 130AD. There are more than 5,000 Greek manuscripts, 10,000 Latin manuscripts and 9,300 other manuscripts, plus over 36,000 citings in other early Christian writings. The great textural critic FJA Hort wrote:

'In the variety and fullness of the evidence on which it rests, the text of the New Testament stands absolutely and unapproachably alone among ancient prose writing.'[7]

FF Bruce summarises the evidence by quoting Sir Frederick Kenyon, a leading scholar in this area:

'*The interval then between the dates and the original composition and the earliest external evidence becomes so small as to be in fact negligible, and thus the last foundation for any doubt the Scriptures have come down to us substantially as they were written have now been removed. Both the authenticity and the general integrity of the books of the New Testament may be regarded as finally established.*'[8]

The writings of FF Bruce and these other Biblical scholars show the texts of the New Testament are accurate and reliable. By believing the accounts that are written in the four Gospels it will help establish an accurate timeframe of events for the final twenty-four hours in the earthly life of Jesus Christ, the Son of God, who is God.

Let's begin our quest to establish an accurate chronology of events of Jesus' final hours with his arrival at the Upper Room in Jerusalem:

18:20-19:00

18:20 Hours

Jesus arrived at the Upper Room

Mark 14:17 says Jesus and his disciples arrived at the Upper Room in Jerusalem as evening came. Evenings begin at sunset. The solar calendar for Jerusalem says the sun sets at 18:20 Hours[a] at the time of Passover in the current year. The time of sunsets is unchanged over the years. If it sets at that time today, then it would have set at 18:20 Hours on the day before Jesus, God's Son died on the cross. Jesus would have arrived at the Upper Room after 18:20 Hours.

18:20 Hours to 18:50 Hours

Jesus washed his disciples' feet

As the meal was being served, Jesus showed his disciples (including Judas) the full extent of his love. He rose from the table, took off his robe, wrapped a towel around his waist and washed his disciples' feet, drying them with the towel. Simon asked him if he was going to wash his feet. He replied, "*You do not realise now what I am doing, but later you will understand.*" His refusal to let Jesus wash his feet showed both his pride and his lack of understanding of Jesus and his mission. When Jesus said, "*Unless I wash you, you have no part with me,*" Simon told him to wash his head and hands as well. Jesus said that those who have had a bath need only to wash their feet as their whole body was clean. He added they were clean, but not every one of them – referring to Judas his betrayer. When he had finished, he said he had set an example for his disciples to follow (John 13:1-17).

18:20 Hours to 18:50 Hours

Jesus' life was a life of service. He gave himself fully to his disciples and to the ever-present crowd of needy people who thronged around him during his ministry. The attitude of the Son of God in human form was one of a humble servant serving the people he came to save. So vital is the servant principle in God's kingdom that at the Last Supper, he gave his disciples, and us a practical demonstration by taking the role of a servant and washing their feet. Jesus is God. He is King of kings and Lord of lords. He is glorious in majesty, might and power, yet he humbled himself and became a man and a servant to all.

In Bible times, people's feet were washed after entering the house. If Jesus arrived at the house after 18:20 Hours, he would have washed his disciples' feet shortly after that time. The meal was being served as he washed them (John 13:2-11). Luke 22:15 says the Last Supper was a Passover meal. Numbers 9:3 say Passover meals begin at twilight. Twilight occurs about half an hour after sunset. On the day before Jesus was crucified, the sun set at 18:20 Hours. If twilight fell half an hour later, it would have happened around 18:50 Hours. He would have washed his disciples' feet from 18:20 to 18:50 Hours.

18:50 Hours

The Last Supper began

As Jesus reclined at the table, he told his disciples he had longed to eat this Passover with them before he suffered (Luke 22:14-16). His own words confirm that the Last Supper was a Passover meal. This meal would have begun at twilight (Numbers 9:3), which fell that day at 18:50 Hours. As the meal began, Jesus poured wine into a cup and gave it his disciples, saying he would not drink it again until his kingdom came (Luke 22:17-18). At a traditional Passover meal the host would say a blessing over the first of four cups of wine served during the meal before passing it to his guests. So Jesus would have served this first cup of wine to his disciples around 18:50 Hours.

19:00-20:00

19:00 Hours to 20:00 Hours

Jesus predicted his betrayal

After washing their feet, he was troubled and said, "*I tell you the truth, one of you is going to betray me.*" (John 13:21). Matthew 26:21-25 and Mark 14:18-21 say Jesus predicted his betrayal as they ate and Luke 22:20-23 says it was after they had finished eating. Luke often placed events earlier or later in a sequence than Matthew and Mark. Luke 8:19-21 says Jesus taught on his true family after he taught the crowds in parables. Matthew 12:46-50 and Mark 3:31-35 say it was before. Luke 18:35-43 says Jesus healed Bartimaeus as he entered Jericho on his final journey. Matthew 20:29-34 and Mark 10:46-52 say it was as he left Jericho. If Luke moved this event, Jesus would have predicted his betrayal as they ate. The Last Supper was a Passover meal. It would have started at twilight (Numbers 9:3), at 18:50 Hours.

When his disciples heard Jesus say that one of them would betray him, they were all saddened and stared at one another, at a loss to know which of them he meant. They began to say to Jesus one after the other, "*Surely not I, Lord?*" When Judas asked this, Jesus said "*You yourself have said it.*" (Matthew 26:20-25). It appears that the other disciples did not hear Jesus say this to Judas, so he must have been sitting near to or next to him. Peter motioned to John, who was reclining next to Jesus to ask him who it was. Jesus told John that his betrayer would be the one to whom he gave the piece of bread that he was holding. Then Jesus dipped the piece of bread into a bowl of 'charoseth paste' and gave it to Judas Iscariot. As soon as Judas took the piece of bread, Satan entered into him (John 13:21-27).

15

19:00 Hours to 20:00 Hours

About halfway through a Passover meal, which celebrated Israel's exodus from Egypt, the host (in this case Jesus), washed his hands for a second time and filled some unleavened bread with some of the Passover lamb then dipped it in a bowl of 'charoseth paste'. This paste represented the mortar that the Jews used when they made bricks during their time of slavery in Egypt. The host would give this sop or sandwich to his honoured guest seated next to him (in this case Judas Iscariot). If John was seated on Jesus' right then Judas must have been seated on his left. This would explain why the other disciples did not hear Jesus' conversations with Judas.

After Judas was identified as Jesus' betrayer, he left the house and it was night (John 13:21-30). From the time that Jesus arrived in the Upper Room to the time he predicted Judas would betray him, it had turned from evening to night. Night falls about thirty to forty minutes after twilight. If twilight fell that day at around 18:50 Hours, it would have turned to night from 19:20 Hours to 19:30 Hours. Judas Iscariot would have left the house to betray Jesus to the Jewish religious leaders after 19:30 Hours. Judas took the darkness that was inside him into the darkness outside. Interestingly, the only people he spoke to after Satan had entered into him were the Jewish leaders.

The disciples argued about greatness

Luke 22:20-34 says it was after they had finished the eating part of the Last Supper that Jesus predicted Judas' betrayal. Then Luke recorded the disciples argued about who was greatest, before he predicted Peter would deny him. John 13:31-38 says he predicted Peter's denials after Judas left the house, after he was revealed as Jesus' betrayer. Luke followed John's order of events, but he added the disciples argued. It is another example of Luke's style of writing, where he recorded an event later in a sequence of events than the other Gospel writers. Luke did this when he said Jesus taught on his true family after he taught the crowds in parables (Luke 8:19-21).

19:00 Hours to 20:00 Hours

Matthew 26:21-25, Mark 14:18-21 and John 13:21-30 agree Jesus predicted his betrayal as they ate, after which he predicted Peter's denials (John 13:31-38) and his disciples argued. They were looking ahead to a glorious kingdom without considering the trials, suffering and service that preceded such an elevation to glory. Yet, Jesus did not rebuke them, but patiently explained that the greatest among them would be the one who served and commended their faithfulness to him (Luke 22:24-30). Luke placed this event after the meal. If he moved the prediction of Jesus' betrayal to after the meal then he could have changed the timing of the disciples arguing about who was greatest. It could have happened before the meal began and Jesus washed their feet to demonstrate to them the true nature of serving. If not, the disciples would have argued about greatness after Judas left the house after 19:30 Hours and possibly before 20:00 Hours.

Jesus predicted Peter's denials

Luke 22:31-34 and John 13:31-38 say that Jesus predicted Peter would deny him during the Last Supper. However, Matthew 26:30-35 and Mark 14:26-31 say it happened as Jesus and his disciples walked to the Mount of Olives after the meal. For the Gospel accounts to agree, Jesus must have predicted Peter's denials twice that night. If the first time was during the Last Supper, it would have taken place in the same timeframe as his disciples argued about who was greatest, that is from 19:30 Hours to 20:00 Hours. Jesus said, *"Simon, Simon, Satan has asked to sift you as wheat. But I have prayed for you, Simon that your faith may not fail. And when you have turned back, strengthen your brothers."* (Luke 22:31-32). He was warning Peter that the Devil wanted to crush them to show their faith was not wheat, but chaff, which would be blown away in the wind of testing. Jesus reassured him that he had prayed for him and the others that their faith would not fail. He was telling them they would be tested and they would fail. The good news was, they would be restored. And once Peter was restored, he was to strengthen the other disciples.

19:00 Hours to 20:00 Hours

Interestingly, Jesus called him, 'Simon.' This was his natural name – his birth name. It was not the name Jesus had given him – 'Peter', the name on which Jesus would build his Church. Jesus would have said this to show Peter it would be his earthly nature that would cause him to fail. Despite this clear warning, Peter did not take heed. In fact, he refuted Jesus' words and boasted he was ready to go to prison with him and even to death. He was so confident of his love and loyalty to Jesus that there was no possibility in his mind that he would not stand by him in all circumstances, even if it meant going to prison or death. Peter thought he knew better than God. How wrong he was!

Jesus told Peter, "*I tell you Peter, before the rooster crows today, you will deny three times that you know me.*" Out of his great love for Peter, Jesus was preparing him for the trials and heartache that lay ahead. Peter's pride stopped him humbling himself and heeding his words. Peter was insulted by what Jesus said and, in his heart, he rebelled against what he heard. Peter's pride stopped him from hearing and responding correctly to Jesus' words of warning. As Peter looked in his heart, he saw only his loyalty and devotion to Jesus. He completely overlooked his human frailty, which would be fully revealed in the next few hours. And it was not just Peter who trusted in his own human strength and wherewithal that night. All of the other disciples also vowed to stand with Jesus in all his trials and would even go do death with him. Jesus would have predicted that Peter would deny him three times from 19:30 Hours to 20:00 Hours.

20:00-21:00

20:00 Hours to 21:00 Hours

Jesus introduced the New Covenant

Whilst they were eating, Jesus took bread and gave thanks then he broke it and gave it to his disciples, saying, *"Take and eat; this is my body given for you; do this in remembrance of me."* Then Jesus took the cup, and when he had given thanks, he gave it to them, saying, *"Drink from it, all of you. This is my blood of the new covenant, which is poured out for you and for many, for the forgiveness of sins. I tell you, the truth, I will not drink from this fruit of the vine from now on until that day when I drink it anew with you in my Father's kingdom."* (Matthew 26:26-29; Mark 14:22-25 and Luke 22:19-23).

A traditional Passover meal remembered the Israelites' exodus from Egypt and their forty years of wandering in the desert. Now Jesus was telling his disciples to remember something more important. For three years they had heard his wonderful words and parables and seen all his signs and miracles. Yet he did not tell them to remember any of them. He told them to remember his death on the cross at Calvary. The Son of God, God himself, came to Earth to die for our sins on the cross. His death frees us from our sins. His death gives us eternal life. His death heals us from all our sicknesses and diseases. His death redeems us from all the power of the curse that fell on man after Adam fell in Eden. His death restores to us all that was lost in the Fall. His death restores our relationship with God. Jesus' death – this one single action achieves all this and so much more. It is why he wanted his disciples and us to remember his death above all else – What a wonderful Saviour! What a loving, forgiving God we have!

19

20:00 Hours to 21:00 Hours

When Jesus instituted the New Covenant, he broke bread and gave a piece to each of the disciples. He was demonstrating to them that they were all part of his body. And so are we. His death on the cross makes us one with himself and God. When God made the first covenant with the Israelites at Mount Sinai in the Exodus from Egypt, the covenant was sealed with blood – the blood of animals. The New Covenant between God and man was sealed also with blood – the blood of Jesus Christ, His Son, the blood he shed for our sins on the cross. The red wine in the Communion Cup is a continual reminder to us of the eternal covenant between God and man – the forgiveness of our sins through the shed blood of His Son, Jesus.

Cups of wine served at the Last Supper

Four cups of wine are served at a Passover meal and Luke 22:14-20 recorded the drinking of two of those four cups at the Last Supper. The first was after Jesus said he had longed to eat this meal with his disciples. It seems Luke recorded the serving of the first of the four cups of wine served that night. The second cup Luke recorded was as Jesus instituted the New Covenant after they had finished eating.

At a Passover meal, the second cup of wine is served before the meal and the third is served soon after it. It suggests Luke recorded the third cup. At a traditional Passover meal, it was served with bread and the words, '*this is the bread of affliction our fathers ate when they came out of Egypt*'[9]. It seems Jesus changed the usual words that night to, '*This is my body given for you. Do this in remembrance of me!*'[10] He instituted the New Covenant after predicting his betrayal and Peter's denials. It would have happened after 20:00 Hours and before Jesus and the disciples left the Upper Room, in the period from 20:00 Hours to 21:00 Hours. If it was the third cup of wine that Jesus served as he instituted the New Covenant then Judas Iscariot must have left the house after the second cup of wine had been served and played no part in the New Covenant of Jesus' body and blood.

20:00 Hours to 21:00 Hours

Jesus and his disciples sang a hymn

Matthew 26:30 and Mark 14:26 say that the last thing Jesus and his disciples did before they left the Upper Room to go to the Mount of Olives was to sing a hymn. Singing a hymn was the penultimate part of a traditional Passover meal. They would have sung a hymn after Jesus had instituted the New Covenant of his body and blood with the third of the four cups of wine served at the meal that night. The fourth cup of wine would have been served before they sang a hymn. If he instituted the New Covenant of his body and blood after 20:00 Hours then Jesus and his disciples would have sung the hymn after that time and possibly before 21:00 Hours.

Jesus is the way, the truth and the life

John 14:1-17:26 says after Jesus predicted Peter's denials, he told his disciples he is the way, the truth and the life. Then he promised to send them the Holy Spirit and said he was the True Vine before telling them the world would hate them because it had hated him. Next, he told them of the work of the Holy Spirit before he prayed for himself, his disciples and for all who would believe in him. Then John 18:1 says after he had finished praying they left for the Mount of Olives. These events would have happened after Jesus and his disciples had sung a hymn and before they left the house in Jerusalem.

The first thing, Jesus taught his disciples was that he was returning to his Father's house to prepare a place for them and he would come back to take them with him so they could be where he was. When he said they knew the way to the place where he was going, Thomas said they did not know where he was going, so how could they know the way. Jesus replied, "*I am the way, the truth and the life and no one comes to the Father except through me.*" Jesus is the only way to God. He is the truth about God and he is the life of God. Fullness of life and eternal life are found only in Jesus Christ, God's Son.

20:00 Hours to 21:00 Hours

Jesus told his disciples that if they really knew him, they would know his Father too. When he said they did know his Father and had seen him, Philip asked him to show them his Father as that would be enough for them. Jesus said anyone who had seen him had seen the Father. His words and the miracles he had performed was his Father working in him. He added that anyone who believed in him would do even greater things than he had done, because he was going to the Father. He promised to do whatever they asked in his name so he could glorify his Father (John 14:1-14). One thing the disciples did know was that Jesus was leaving them, but they did not understand how or why. He comforted them and encouraged them to put their trust in God – for God never fails. If Jesus is the way then we know the destination, because he came from the Father who is in heaven and he came to show us his Father. Jesus would have said, "I am the way, the truth and the life," after 20:00 Hours and before 21:00 Hours.

Jesus promised the Holy Spirit

Then Jesus promised he would ask his Father to send his disciples another counsellor to be with them forever— the Spirit of Truth, who would live in them. Jesus said he would not abandon them. Though the world would not see him anymore, they would see him. Jesus said that anyone who loved him would obey his teaching. His Father would love him, and they would come and make their home with him. He said God would send the Holy Spirit in his name and he would teach them all things and would remind them of everything Jesus had told them. But the world had to learn Jesus loved his Father; and he did exactly what his Father had told him. Then Jesus told his disciples they must obey his commands (John 14:15-31). Obedience is the key to the Christian life and on it hangs our security, love and peace. Then Jesus said, "*let us leave*!" If they were ready to leave the house then the Last Supper must have ended. He would have promised to send them the Holy Spirit after 20:00 Hours and before 21:00 Hours.

20:00 Hours to 21:00 Hours

Jesus told his disciples he was the True Vine

After Jesus had promised to send the Holy Spirit, he told his disciples he was the True Vine and his Father was the gardener, who cut off every branch in him that did not bear fruit, whilst every branch that did bear fruit he pruned, so it would be even more fruitful. Jesus told them, if they did not remain in him they could not bear fruit by themselves. Then he said he was the Vine and they were the branches. Apart from Jesus, his disciples could do nothing. Yet, if they remained in him and his words remained in them then they could ask for anything in his name and it would be done for them.

We are dependent on Jesus for our life. Without him we can do nothing. Also we are interdependent with one another. The Church of Jesus Christ is rooted and grounded in him, with his life flowing through us to produce life and fruit. The fruit his disciples bore would be for his Father's glory and it would show the world that they were disciples of Jesus. Then the Lord told them that they would remain in his love if they kept his commands. He commanded them to love one another as he had loved them. He said the greatest demonstration of love was to lay down one's life for one's friends (John 15:1-17). Jesus would have said this from 20:00 Hours to 21:00 Hours.

The world would hate Jesus' disciples

John 15:18-16:4 says after Jesus said, "*I am the true vine!*" He told his disciples that the world would hate them, because it had hated him. However, they no longer belonged to the world as he had chosen them out of the world. His disciples would be treated this way because of Jesus' name. It showed the people did not know him or the Father who had sent him. Jesus added the people had seen his miracles, yet they had hated both him and his Father, which fulfilled the Scripture, '*They hated me without reason*' (Psalm 69:4). Jesus would have said this between 20:00 Hours and 21:00 Hours.

20:00 Hours to 21:00 Hours

Jesus taught on the work of the Holy Spirit

After Jesus told his disciples the world would hate them, he taught them on the work of the Holy Spirit. He said if he did not go away the Holy Spirit would not come to them. When He came, He would convict the world of guilt about sin and righteousness and judgment: about sin because men did not believe in him; about righteousness, because Jesus was going to the Father, where the disciples could see him no longer; and about judgment, because the Prince of this world, the Devil now stood condemned (John 16:5-11). The Spirit of truth would guide them into all truth and would tell them what was to come. He would bring glory to Jesus by taking from what was his and making it known to his disciples (John 16:12-15).

Then Jesus told them that in a little while they would see him no more (after his death) and after a little while they would see him (after his resurrection). When his disciples did not understand, Jesus explained the pain they would experience at his death and the joy they would experience at his resurrection. He added that his heavenly Father loved them because they had loved him and He would give them whatever they asked for in his name. When Jesus said that he had come from the Father and he was returning to his Father then his disciples believed that Jesus had come from God. It caused Jesus to declare, "*You believe at last!*" (John 16:16-33). The Lord would have taught on the work of the Holy Spirit from 20:00 Hours to 21:00 Hours.

21:00-22:00

21:00 Hours to 22:00 Hours

Jesus prayed for himself

After Jesus taught on the work of the Holy Spirit, he prayed for himself. He asked his Father to glorify him so that he could glorify his Father. In humility, Jesus sought to glorify his Father. It had been his intention from the time his ministry began and it was his intention as it came to an end. Then Jesus declared his God-given authority to grant eternal life to those his Father had given him. He defined eternal life as believers knowing his Father, the only true God and his Son, Jesus Christ, whom He had sent (John 17:1-5). Eternal life could only be available to repentant sinners when the crucified Son of God had risen from the dead and ascended to his former glory at his Father's right hand in heaven. Jesus was determined the work his heavenly Father had given him to do should be seen through to the end.

Jesus prayed for his disciples

Jesus' love for his disciples was shown when he prayed for them. He asked his Father to protect them from the Devil by the power of the name He had given him – Jesus. He asked God to keep them united; to sanctify them by His word and to let them be filled with the fullness of his joy (John 17:6-19). It is the prayer of our great High Priest as he interceded for his disciples and it is the prayer of a man praying for his beloved friends. For over three years he had faithfully given them the teaching his Father had given him. During that time, he had protected them and kept them safe before he sent them out as apostles into the world. Apostles means sent ones.

25

21:00 Hours to 22:00 Hours

Jesus prayed for all believers

After Jesus had prayed for himself and for his disciples, he prayed for all who would believe in him (John 17:20-26). This is the prayer Jesus prayed for us. His will was always to do his Father's will. He and his Father always moved together, worked together, and communicated with each other constantly. They had the same love and the same goal. This is how the fellowship between believers in Jesus Christ the Son of God should be. This is how believers in the Church of Christ should be. This is what Jesus prayed for when he asked his Father that believers may be one just as he and his Father are one. Believers in Jesus can only be one with one another as far as they are one with God and to the degree that His love is in them. Then the world will know we are the children of the living God. John 17:1-26 recorded the three prayers just before Jesus and his disciples left the Upper Room. If Jesus walked to the Garden of Gethsemane from 21:30 Hours to 22:00 Hours (see below) then he would have prayed these three prayers just before they left the house.

The disciples found two swords

Before leaving the Upper Room, Jesus asked his disciples if they lacked anything when he had sent them out to preach and heal, without purse, bag, or sandals (Mark 6:6-13). They replied they had lacked nothing. Jesus told them, if they had a purse they were to take it and also a bag. He added that if they did not possess a sword they should sell their cloak and buy one. Jesus said this so the Scripture would be fulfilled, '*And he was numbered with the transgressors*' (Isaiah 53:12). Then Jesus told his disciples that everything that had been written about him was reaching its fulfilment. Then his disciples told Jesus that they had found two swords (Luke 22:35-38). If they walked to Gethsemane on the Mount of Olives from 21:30 Hours to 22:00 Hours (see below) then they would have found the swords just before they left the house in Jerusalem.

21:00 Hours to 22:00 Hours

Journey to Gethsemane

Christian tradition says the house where Jesus ate the Last Supper was near the palace of the high priest. If that is correct, Jesus and his disciples would have descended from the Upper Room into the street and headed east towards the Mount of Olives. They would have passed near the high priest's palace as they walked through Jerusalem's narrow streets. After crossing the Tyropean valley that split the city in two, they would have exited the city through the Fountain Gate and descended into the Kidron valley (John 18:1). They would have headed north along the path that ran along the base of the deep gorge that separates the city on the west from the Mount of Olives on the east. At a point opposite the temple, they would have turned right and ascended the slopes of the Mount of Olives then entered the Garden of Gethsemane on the lower slope of the hill. It would have taken them about half an hour to get there[11]. If Jesus and his disciples arrived at Gethsemane at 22:00 Hours (see below), they would have left the house at 21:30 Hours after the Last Supper.

Jesus predicted Peter's denials

On the way to Gethsemane (21:30-22:00 Hours), Matthew 26:31-35 and Mark 14:27-31 say Jesus said all of his disciples would abandon him and he made no exceptions. Peter said, if all the others deserted Jesus, he never would and added he was willing to die with him. The others said the same. Then Jesus predicted Peter would deny him for the second time that night. The first time was during the Last Supper (Luke 22:31-34 and John 13:31-38). Peter was willing to put down the others to swear his loyalty and devotion to Jesus. He should have known, '*A haughty sprit goes before a fall!*' (Proverb 16:18). Peter's love and zeal for him was admirable, but his pride was not. He was offended by Jesus' words and was belligerent to him. He added he was not only more dependable than the other disciples, he was more dependable than anyone else, "*If all fall away, I never will!*"

21:00 Hours to 22:00 Hours

When the personal pronoun is over present then pride is the voice behind it. Because of Peter's pride, God allowed him to fall – just far enough to learn humility. One cannot doubt that Peter was sincere. The problem was he was sincerely wrong. In his own heart, he could not comprehend he would ever deny Jesus. He was sincerely wrong about his assessment of himself and his own strength. He was slow to look at his own weaknesses, but quick to look at the weaknesses in the other disciples and highlight them to make himself look better in front of Jesus. He made a huge mistake comparing himself to others when the perfect man was standing before him. If he had compared himself to Jesus, he would have had a true assessment of himself.

Peter's problem was he did not really know himself. He thought he did, but he did not and soon he would learn that truth. Jesus knew exactly who he was. He was a perfect man. He did not think too highly or too lowly of himself. He knew himself fully and that night gave himself fully to God. He was fully God and fully man and gave the fully man side of himself fully to God that night. Peter had no such balanced view of himself. He thought too highly of himself. His overconfidence in himself caused him to fall. Peter believed he had the power and strength in and of himself to stand for and with Jesus, come what may. He did not understand the weakness of his flesh.

In his pride and self-righteousness, Peter believed he was above serious sin and minimised even the words of Jesus, who prophesied he would fail. Peter refuted Jesus' words, "No! Absolutely not! It is not going to happen!" he boasted. Peter was depending on himself, but needed to depend on God – for everything. In the house, Jesus warned Peter and the others about this when he said he was the Vine and they could do nothing without him. He continued to encourage them on the way to Gethsemane, but his words fell on deaf ears.

22:00-23:00

22:00 Hours to 23:00 Hours

Jesus' first prayer

The Garden of Gethsemane was a place Jesus knew well. It was his haven on his visits to Jerusalem during his ministry. There, he told his disciples, "*Sit here while I go over there and pray!*" He took Peter, James and John along with him and began to be sorrowful, deeply distressed and troubled. He said to them, "*My soul is exceedingly sorrowful, even to the point of death. Stay here and keep watch with me!*" Going a little further he fell with his face to the ground, praying, "*My Father, everything is possible for you. If it is possible; may this cup be taken from me? Yet not what I will, but what you will. Not my will, but your will be done.*" (Matthew 26:36-39 and Mark 14:32-36).

In Gethsemane, the pain and anguish of the violent ordeal, Jesus would soon endure as he suffered and died on a cross for the sins of the world weighed heavily on him. He told his disciples his soul was filled with sorrow to the point of death. He was overwhelmed at the thought of the tremendous suffering that lay ahead. With the weight of death heavily upon him, Jesus recoiled at the idea of subjecting himself to so violent and painful a death. After expressing feelings of distress and revulsion to his disciples, Jesus expressed them to his Father in prayer. He asked God to take the cup from him – the cup being the awaiting ordeal of pain, suffering and death. When the cup of suffering was held out for Jesus to drink, he agonised to grasp it. At that moment, doing God's will was painfully difficult for Jesus as he struggled greatly before God to face his God-given destiny.

22:00 Hours to 23:00 Hours

In his first prayer, Jesus for the first time in his ministry and in his life made a distinction between his will and his Father's will, '*not what I will, but what you will and not my will, but your will be done.*' His life had been dependent on the will of his Father. He even said his food was to do the will of his Father (John 4:34). Throughout his ministry Jesus and his Father's will had always been one. In Gethsemane that night, he was making a distinction – '*I will*' and '*my will.*' He sent up a cry to his Father from a soul flooded with anguish, torment and fear. Jesus bared his soul to his Father in an expression of his natural abhorrence of the awful fate, which weighed heavily on him.

He prayed for the cup to be taken away from him then said, "*Not my will be done, but Father, your will be done!*" (Mark 14:36). He prayed God would not answer his prayer according to Jesus' will, but according to His will. He was prepared God could deny his request and was willing to submit to God's will. However great his desire to avoid suffering and death, Jesus was aware there was a greater will than his to which he must submit. He was open to his fragility as a human and open to God's will even though it went against his own, as he communicated with his Father in openness and intimacy.

Jesus called on divine power to enable him to do what was humanly impossible. He recognised he was at the end of his human resources. He had no power of his own and opened himself up to God's power. Without that power, he was unable to drink the cup God had placed before him. He could not face death or renounce power over his own life (the power of self-preservation). Only God's power could enable him to do so. Only God can enable human beings to follow a path of selfless sacrifice, self-giving and suffering. Jesus asked for the cup to be taken from him. He is fully God and fully man. As man he had a human will and natural inclinations, which he resisted up to this point in his life as he executed his Father's will. That night, in Gethsemane, Jesus, God's Son showed the full extent of his humanity.

22:00 Hours to 23:00 Hours

Jesus did not ask his Father absolutely, he asked him conditionally. He did not tell Him to take the cup away, he asked Him to take it away, but not as he willed; as his Father willed. Jesus submitted himself to his Father's will. In this familiar, friendly place, he experienced the greatest agony, anguish and loneliness anyone has ever known. He was feeling the weight of the sins of the world and wrestling with Satan's temptation not to go through with it. Despite all of this, Jesus' one desire was to do his Father's will. However, it was not an easy thing to do. It took a tremendous, spiritual, emotional, mental and physical struggle to achieve it. And Jesus' first prayer that night was just the first part of that struggle in Gethsemane.

Jesus found his disciples asleep

When Jesus had finished his first prayer he found Peter, James and John asleep. He asked Peter why he could not keep watch for one hour (Mark 14:37). Jesus' words reveal his first prayer lasted an hour. If they arrived in the Garden of Gethsemane at 22:00 Hours, his first prayer began then and ended at 23:00 Hours. Then Jesus told his three disciples, "*Watch and pray so you will not fall into temptation. The spirit is willing, but the flesh is weak.*" (Mark 14:38).

He had warned his disciples about the trials they faced at the Last Supper and on the way to Gethsemane. Now in the garden Jesus encouraged them to, "Keep watch!" They had to be vigilant for the trials that lay ahead. He told them to pray so they would not fall into temptation (Mark 14:38), because the spirit was willing, but the flesh was weak. He knew they needed God's strength and not their own to get through their trials. He advised them what to do and had shown this truth to them in that first hour, as he agonised in the garden. If the Son of God needed to pray to his Father for the strength to face his ordeal then so did his disciples. Peter and the other disciples would have heard Jesus pray those words before they fell asleep. However, they had not taken in the truth and the gravity of his words.

22:00 Hours to 23:00 Hours

Despite finding Peter, James and John asleep when they should have been keeping watch over him, Jesus in his love told them what they needed to do to face their ordeal. He told them to put their confidence and trust in God and not in themselves and their own strength. They had displayed their self-declared dependability. They needed to learn the humility and poverty of spirit needed for God to work through them. He encouraged them with understanding words, *"The spirit is willing, but the flesh is weak!"* He knew they desired to do what was right, but they displayed the weakness common to all humanity.

Man, in his nature lacks the discipline and strength to live up to his highest desires. God understands our dilemma. He remembers we are weak and frail in our human selves. Jesus understood why his disciples had failed him in not staying awake to keep watch over him as he had told them. He spent that hour alone, prostrate in prayer. Though they spent that hour prostrate in sleep, he encouraged them to watch and pray as it is the only way through trials. Good will and good intentions can come to nothing in trials through human weakness. It happened to the disciples. He told them to pray so they might have God's power to get through the ordeal. Jesus did not tell them to do anything he did not do. It was the prayer he had prayed.

When it came to facing the realities of suffering and death, Jesus and his disciples are shown to be equally vulnerable and weak. They were deluded about their own strength and power. Jesus faced his vulnerabilities and confronted his convulsion at the prospect of pain and dying, as he acknowledged his own fears and fragility. They denied theirs, as they lacked self-knowledge. As a result, they could not support him as he prayed. Instead of watching over Jesus, they slept, as he struggled in prayer, alone. He had asked them to watch, but they had failed. If Jesus prayed for an hour after arriving in the garden at 22:00 Hours, he would have woken them at 23:00 Hours.

23:00-24:00

23:00 Hours to 24:00 Hours

Jesus' second prayer

After finding his disciples asleep the first time, Jesus went away and prayed a second time. Mark 14:39 says he prayed the same thing as the first time. Matthew 26:42 records his words, "*My Father, if it is not possible for this cup to be taken away unless I drink it, may your will be done!*" In his second prayer there is no mention of his own will as there had been in his first prayer. He mentioned only his Father's will. If He did not want the cup to be taken away then he wanted God's will to be done. In this prayer, he surrendered and yielded to God's will.

As God and man, Jesus had both a human will and a divine will. He said it himself, '*my will.*' When he told his Father, "*Your will be done!*" he accepted unequivocally and unconditionally the chalice of his pain, suffering and death on a cross. He accepted it in his divine will when he left heaven's throne and came to Earth as a man. In the garden, he submitted to this in his human will. He had to experience death within so he could experience it without. He had to face death on the inside to face death on the outside. His will and spirit had to die on the inside before he could physically die on the outside. His suffering and death were divinely ordained to save sinful man. He submitted his will in selfless love and humble obedience. In the Garden of Gethsemane, he dealt with the forthcoming suffering and death he would experience as a man. Everything in Jesus' human nature cried out against it. This part of his human spirit and will had to submit fully to God's sovereign will, if he was to see his suffering and death through to the end. Only a fully submitted human will could do that.

23:00 Hours to 24:00 Hours

It was fully natural for Jesus to abhor the idea of his suffering. Every fibre in his human being shrank from being: betrayed; deserted; spat on; punched; slapped; imprisoned; having a crown of thorns impaled on his head; being repeatedly struck with a staff; being flogged; having nails driven into his hands and feet; hanging on a cross in excruciating pain as his blood and life drained out of him; being mocked; and insulted; before being abandoned by his heavenly Father; and dying alone on the cross of Calvary. It is a natural instinct to hate pain and suffering and to fear death and try to avoid it, if possible. We all have a natural aversion to pain. Jesus who is fully human had those instincts. In fact, the greatest battle in man's relationship with God is his total submission of his human spirit, that is, his human will to the sovereignty and will of God. As man, he did this. He showed us it is possible and he showed us how to do it, in his agonising in prayer in the garden, he did not reach that level of submission after his first prayer, which lasted an hour (22:00 Hours to 23:00 Hours). God's Son in human form agonised in prayer for another hour after it (from 23:00 to 24:00 Hours).

Jesus found his disciples asleep

After Jesus finished praying the second time, he found Peter, James and John asleep because their eyes were heavy. When he woke them, they did not know what to say to him (Mark 14:40). It is interesting that just a short while ago, when Peter saw Jesus in his most divine state when he was transfigured on the mountain, he could not stop talking (Luke 9:28-36). However, that night in the Garden of Gethsemane on the Mount of Olives, when Peter saw Jesus in his most human state, as he agonised in prayer, he was too embarrassed to say anything. If Jesus' second prayer began at 23:00 Hours and it ended one hour later at midnight, he would have found his disciples asleep at 24:00 Hours.

00:00-01:00

00:00 Hours to 01:00 Hours

Jesus' third prayer

After Jesus found his disciples asleep following his second prayer, he went away and prayed the same thing a third time. He prayed, "*My Father, if it is not possible for this cup to be taken away unless I drink it, may your will be done*" (Matthew 26:42-44). The struggle that had been in his heart in his first two prayers continued in his third prayer. Jesus' repeated acts of submission to the will of God in his first two prayers had not destroyed completely the opposition his human will and human nature felt to his forthcoming humiliation, pain, suffering and death. The intensity in Jesus' soul was mounting and he prayed more earnestly. He prayed from the supreme anguish that gripped his soul, in the struggle to submit his natural inclinations to God's will and accept all the pain and suffering of his Passion.

Even before he prayed, Jesus said his soul was overwhelmed with grief to the point of death. After he expressed his submission and his acceptance of the cup of his suffering and death, his anguish did not subside. It went on increasing until it reached a climax as his inner struggle produced an outflow of sweat, like blood (Luke 22:39-44). His suffering was concentrated in his soul and overflowed into his body, distressing and weakening it. God sent an angel to give him strength in both his body and soul. After the angel came the intensity of Jesus' prayer increased. It was the culminating point in his mental, emotional and spiritual suffering. Jesus prayed more earnestly and as a result of the racking interior anguish, his sweat was like blood.

00:00 Hours to 01:00 Hours

If Jesus' sweat was mixed with blood then the violence of the conflict in his soul manifested itself outwardly in bloody sweat. His blood was forced from its vessels through pores to the surface of his skin. As it mixed with his sweat it formed into thick drops that fell to the floor. As a result of his prayers, peace reigned in his heart. He clearly saw the path that lay before him and it was the way of the cross. Now he was ready and willing. With complete and detailed foreknowledge of what awaited him, Jesus walked deliberately to the cross of Calvary.

Jesus is God and man. No suffering, exterior or interior could reach him unless he permitted it. Whatever he suffered in the garden, he allowed himself to suffer. He opened wide the floodgates of his soul and gave entry to the torrent of fear, abhorrence, disgust and sorrow that weighed on him. He allowed this suffering of his soul to show how human he is, to give us courage in our fears. He set an example to reveal the grace we need for our own interior conflicts. That night he experienced feelings of sorrow, weariness and disgust. Jesus had clothed himself with flesh to conquer the flesh in its own domain. He feared, but in an anguished internal struggle, he conquered fear as he declared his acceptance of his Father's will. Jesus reached the point where he realised that all his human resources had come to an end.

To deepen our relationship with God and grow spiritually, we must see we can do nothing in our own strength. We do this by imitating Jesus' openness and self-awareness. An honest self-awareness is key to a deeper relationship with God and an ongoing conversion of the heart that leads to a deeper spirituality. Jesus looked his human frailty in the face and dealt with it by submitting it to God. God loves us and is aware of all our frailties. He wants us, like his Son to cast our frailties on Him. Our pride, ego, self-righteousness, stubbornness of will and independence of spirit stops us doing this. God sees past that and loves past the facade we put up in life. Like Jesus we must let go of it all and give it all to God in humble submission.

00:00 Hours to 01:00 Hours

The human heart, mind, soul, body and life are at their most perfect when fully surrendered and submitted to God. In Gethsemane that night, Jesus showed it was by honest self-assessment and open communication with God that the human will and spirit can submit to God. If he could submit everything to God's will to receive the strength needed to get through the intolerable pain and the excruciating death that lay ahead, then we too can submit everything to God and receive the strength to get through any crisis in life – knowing fully, it can never be as painful or as horrific as the one that Jesus suffered.

Mark 14:35-39 says Jesus' first prayer lasted an hour then after he woke his disciples, he prayed the same thing a second time. After he found his disciples asleep the second time, Matthew 26:43-44 says Jesus went away again and prayed the same thing a third time. If his first two prayers each lasted for one hour then his third prayer would have lasted for one hour. Jesus would have begun praying at midnight and his prayer would have ended at 01:00 Hours. He would have prayed for a total of three hours in the Garden of Gethsemane.

Jesus found his disciples asleep

After his third prayer, Jesus found his three disciples asleep again. He asked, *"Are you still sleeping and resting? Look the hour is near and the Son of Man is betrayed into the hands of sinners. Rise. Let's go! Here comes my betrayer!"* (Mark 14:41-42). They did not watch and pray and fell into temptation as a consequence. Jesus used his time in the garden in a disciplined and meaningful way – talking with his Father as he prepared himself for his indescribable suffering and death. Peter, James and John spent that time asleep. They served their human needs and not their spiritual needs. If they had served the latter by watching and praying, it would have met their human needs and they would have had the strength to face the ordeals they were about to go through. They were confident their own strength and devotion to Jesus would see them through, but they were wrong.

00:00 Hours to 01:00 Hours

They should have known Jesus knew their hearts better than they did and heeded his warnings and taken his advice, especially Peter. From the time he called him, Jesus had shown, he knew more than Peter about the things he knew best, such as fishing. Jesus showed it when he provided Peter with a net-breaking, boat-sinking catch of fish on the lake where he fished each day and in a part of it and at a time when catching fish was impossible (Luke 5:1-11). Yet, Peter did not apply that experience to events in the Garden of Gethsemane. He should have reacted that night as he did that day by the Sea of Galilee and humbled himself rather than trying to prove Jesus wrong. It was a decision that was to prove very painful for Peter that night. After he woke him for the third time, he had nothing to say. If his third prayer began at midnight and it ended at 01:00 Hours, he would have awoken Peter and the others at 01:00 Hours.

01:00-02:00

01:00 Hours to 02:00 Hours

Jesus' betrayal and arrest

As Jesus spoke to his disciples after his third prayer, Judas arrived with soldiers, guards and others sent by the Jewish religious leaders. Jesus asked, *"Who is it you want?"* *"Jesus of Nazareth,"* they replied. When he said, *"I am he,"* they drew back and fell to the ground. Again he asked them, *"Who is it you want?"* "Jesus of Nazareth," they said. He replied, *"I told you, I am he. If you are looking for me, let these men go,"* which fulfilled the words, *"I have not lost one of those you gave me."* (John 18:2-9). Then Judas, who had arranged to identify Jesus by kissing him stepped forward. Jesus asked Judas. *"Are you betraying the Son of Man with a kiss?"* (Luke 22:47-48).

This was the second time that the Jewish religious leaders had sent guards to arrest Jesus. The first time was at the Feast of Tabernacles in his final year of ministry (John 7:32-52). On that occasion they had failed. This time they came armed with a crowd in the dead of night when only his disciples were with Jesus. They could not have taken Jesus captive unless he willingly gave himself up to them. He stepped forward and identified himself to them whilst protecting his disciples. This selfless act is symbolic of all that Jesus would suffer for us – the beatings, the mocking and ridicule, the pain and finally, death. Jesus accepted what was coming to him in obedience to his Father's will. When Judas arrived in the Garden of Gethsemane with the mob of armed soldiers, guards and others, the time to drink God's cup had come and Jesus willingly submitted himself to it.

01:00 Hours to 02:00 Hours

Jesus chastised them for coming to arrest him in secret at night with no one around to see. He wanted them to know how hypocritical and wrong they were in arresting him and with such heavy-handedness. They treated Jesus who had never sinned, in whom there was no sin and who did no sin as a criminal and presented themselves as the upright ones and enforcers of the Law. If Jesus had done anything wrong, they could have arrested him any day at the temple. However, it was their hour, the hour of darkness – where the religious leaders were instruments to carry out Satan's will. But Jesus acknowledged it was all part of God's will when he said that their actions fulfilled the Scriptures to bring about the redemption of mankind from sin and sickness and disease and the establishment of the kingdom of God.

His disciples were unable to cope with Jesus' betrayal and arrest. If they had prayed and kept watch as Jesus had told them, God would have given them the wherewithal to cope with these events. They asked Jesus if they should strike those coming to arrest him with their swords. Before he could answer, Peter lashed out with his sword and cut off the ear of the high priest's servant. However, Peter's violent action had no impact on Jesus' arrest. It just showed his lack of understanding of Jesus' mission. He did not need Peter's help in this situation. He had the situation totally under his control. The disciples' lack of understanding led them all to desert Jesus in his hour of need.

They failed him in his need for prayer support then abandoned him totally when he was betrayed and arrested. It was all part of God's will. Jesus had to go to the cross alone. Jesus alone was worthy to suffer and die for our sins. Yet the desertion of his friends must have added to his anguish and sense of loneliness. Despite their boasting, his disciples' frailties had been fully exposed. When the young man fled naked from the garden (Mark 14:51-52), it was a visual depiction of the disciples' frailties. All of them had boasted they would never fall away. Yet, at the first sign of trouble they abandoned Jesus and ran.

01:00 Hours to 02:00 Hours

Events in Gethsemane reveal both Jesus and his disciples' reactions in the time of crisis and the latter fell well short. Jesus faced his own frailties and laid them before God. It was a painful, lonely struggle in the garden for him to reach the point of fully submitting to God's will. The result was that in the heat of the crisis when he called on God's power he had the strength to obey God's will. His disciples denied their frailties as they believed in their own human power to face the crisis and they were the ones exposed as weak and frail. Those who are vulnerable and open are more receptive to themselves and God. His kingdom belongs to such as these, for out of their poverty and weakness they cling to God. The poor in spirit admit they cannot do it on their own and they need God. They know God's power begins when their human resourcefulness ends. Judas and the arresting party arrived in the garden as Jesus woke his disciples after his third prayer (01:00 Hours). It would not have taken long to arrest Jesus – possibly, fifteen minutes. If so, it means he was betrayed, arrested and abandoned by his disciples from 01:00 Hours to 01:15 Hours.

Journey to the high priest

After his arrest, Jesus was bound and led down the slope of the Mount of Olives into the Kidron Valley. The group would have walked south along the path at the base of the valley for fifteen to twenty minutes then turned right and climbed the steep slope up to the city wall. They would have entered Jerusalem though the Fountain Gate and headed north before crossing the Tyropean valley that cut the city in two. After passing the Pool of Siloam, they would have turned west and ascended Jerusalem's narrow streets before arriving at the high priest's palace. It was situated on the slope of the west hill of the city. If the palace was located close to the Upper Room, the journey would have taken the same amount of time it had taken Jesus to walk to Gethsemane – about half an hour[12]. If they left the garden at about 01:15 Hours they would have arrived at the high priest's palace around 01:45 Hours.

01:00 Hours to 02:00 Hours

Jesus' trial by Annas

Jesus was taken to Annas (John 18:13) who had been high priest in Israel. The Romans deposed him in 15AD and made Caiaphas, his son-in-law, high priest instead. The Jews saw it as a lifelong calling and Annas was still held in high honour by them. Annas asked Jesus about his teaching and about his disciples. Jesus told him that he had spoken openly and had always taught in the Jewish synagogues or at the temple in Jerusalem and had said nothing in secret. He suggested that Annas should ask those who had heard him as they knew what he had said. Jesus refused to defend himself or explain his teachings and behaviour to Annas, the high priest, the religious leader of the Jewish people. Truth does not need defending. If Jesus had done wrong, then Annas needed to prove it by following proper procedure.

Basically, Jesus was telling Annas he should do the right thing and produce witnesses if he had a legitimate charge against him and for this trial to be legitimate. As high priest, he should have known and behaved better. He should have been above reproach and followed the judicial procedure rather than try to make Jesus bear witness against himself. Jesus was having none of it and called him to task. He rebuked Israel's leading religious figure without fear or hesitation and Annas was humiliated. He was given a short, sharp lesson on correct legal procedure with a few well-chosen words from Jesus.

Often in life, when the ignorant are faced with a dilemma, they resort to violence and this is what happened that night. An official standing near Jesus struck him in the face. It was cowardly to strike a bound man and it was unjust to treat the accused as a convicted criminal. Jesus looked to Annas to reprove such an aggressive act. When he did nothing, Jesus turned to the one who had struck him and with quiet dignity asked, *"If I have said something wrong then testify to it. If I have not, why did you strike me?"* (John 18:19-24).

01:00 Hours to 02:00 Hours

Jesus reacted to this violence in modesty and meekness. His calm logic was a rebuke to the official who had struck him and to Annas who had permitted it to happen then let it go unpunished. Annas soon realised his line of inquiry was going nowhere and it was making him look bad as the man standing on trial in front of him showed no fear of him. Jesus was not afraid of him. He knew he had to die, no matter what the result of this trial. After praying in anguish for three hours in Gethsemane, where he submitted totally to God's will, he had the strength and inner peace to endure the beginning of his humiliation and suffering. When this trial with Jesus reached an impasse, Annas sent him to be tried by Caiaphas who was the current high priest. During his ordeal, Jesus faced six trials. His trial by Annas was the first of three trials by the religious leaders that he faced. Afterwards Jesus faced three trials by the civil authorities.

In Jewish law, the accused was not obligated to incriminate himself by testifying against himself. Usually, at a trial, the court presented its charges against the accused. Next, the prosecution would present its case through its witnesses. Then the accused would present his defence. After both parties had presented their cases, the judges would assess who had told the truth and would make their judgment.

In this trial, Annas broke every rule of Jewish law. He read no charges to Jesus and produced no witnesses to testify against him. He produced no evidence against Jesus and interrogated him, himself. Annas asked Jesus about his teaching and his disciples, hoping to hear something he had taught in order that he could have a charge against him – be it a religious charge or a political one. Annas was trying to get Jesus to incriminate himself. If Jesus was taken to the palace of the high priest in Jerusalem after he had been arrested in the Garden of Gethsemane then his trial by the former high priest, Annas would have started around 01:45 Hours and it would have continued past 02:00 Hours.

01:00 Hours to 02:00 Hours

Peter's first denial

After Jesus was arrested in Gethsemane and led to Annas' palace, Peter followed at a distance (Luke 22:54). He was safe following at a distance, as he tried to live up to his earlier boasts and promises. He did not follow Jesus and his captors too closely. If he did – if he stood with Jesus as he had promised then he too might lose his life. So Peter struck a balance between the two. He chose the way of compromise and followed Jesus at a distance. Following him, showed Peter had a love for Jesus and a sense of devotion to him. However, his love and devotion were too weak in reality for him to return to the olive grove and stand by Jesus after deserting him. They were only strong enough to follow at a distance. He was still trying to prove his boasts of love and loyalty to Jesus were true. In Peter's mind, following Jesus at a distance showed he was true to his word.

Peter was curious to see what would happen to Jesus. Curiosity, not loyalty got the better of him. Lacking conviction, he acted out of fear. To stand by Jesus would have taken great courage. Peter chose to follow him at a distance. Entering the courtyard of the high priest put him in a perilous environment. His situation was made worse since he had not prepared himself for such a trial. Peter had not watched and prayed as Jesus had instructed him. He lacked the strength needed to stand in the domain of the man determined to kill his Lord. It was presumptive of Peter to place himself in the midst of Jesus' enemies.

He was blind to his weakness and ignorant of the leaders' plans. The stage was set for him to commit the most horrible of sins – to deny Jesus. Events so far revealed Peter's pride and over-confidence and demonstrated his inability and unwillingness to understand himself. They revealed his prayerlessness and independent attitude. He had demonstrated his impulsiveness when he lashed out with his sword then he followed Jesus at a distance to the lion's den of temptation.

01:00 Hours to 02:00 Hours

As Peter entered the courtyard of the high priest's palace, the girl at the gate eyed him. In the shadows of the entrance, she believed he was one of Jesus' disciples. Peter went and warmed himself by the fire in the courtyard. Twice, Mark 14:54 and Mark 14:67 say he sat warming himself by the fire. It implies he thought more of himself and his comfort at that time and less about Jesus' ordeal. The girl from the entrance gate left her post and approached the fire and saw Peter sitting there. She looked intently at him in the firelight, which clearly revealed his features, confirming her earlier suspicions. She boldly went up to him and accused him of being one of Jesus' disciples (Matthew 26:69-70; Mark 14:66-68 and Luke 22:55-57).

Now Peter could stand by his boastful words to Jesus and confirm his love and loyalty to him. Instead, he revealed his lack of moral courage to stand by his own convictions. At the first opportunity big, brash Peter could not stand up to a little servant girl. He failed Jesus and the other disciples when he denied that he knew him or them. John 18:19 says he denied Jesus as he was being tried by Annas. If that trial began at 01:45 Hours, Peter denied Jesus at that time.

Peter's second denial

After denying Jesus the first time, Peter moved from the fire to stand by the entrance gate of the palace courtyard (Matthew 26:71). He withdrew from the light where he could be easily seen to the shadows, close enough to the gate for a quick exit. Peter's actions were a metaphor for what was happening inside him. His lack of watching and praying that night and his reliance on his own strength moved him away from the light to the shadows, where it was neither light nor dark. It was where he was spiritually – a place of compromise. Now he was in a position to save himself and still hear the outcome of Jesus' ordeal. He was still there, showing his love and loyalty to Jesus. He had not deserted him like the others, but he was not standing by him either. To follow Jesus, it must be all or nothing.

01:00 Hours to 02:00 Hours

Peter had failed to keep his words to stand by Jesus and go to death with him. His confidence had diminished and fear filled the vacuum. The effect of his lack of watching and praying was being revealed. He had no strength from God to face this trial. He had enough confidence in himself and his ability to stay in the trial – not in the heat of the fire, but in the cool of the shadows. He compromised commitment for self-preservation, trying to be inconspicuous in the shadows as he stood more in flight than fight mode. The fear filling his heart and soul increased when he was accused a second time of being Jesus' disciple. The girl who had accused him was dissatisfied with his answer and shared her suspicions with others. They came over to Peter and accused him of being a disciple, "*This fellow is one of them!*" When those standing around heard it, they fixed their eyes on Peter. They asked, "*You aren't one of his disciples too, are you?*"

Fearing arrest and even the possibility of death, Peter lashed out in self-defence. He denied any involvement with Jesus – "*I don't know the man!*" To make his argument convincing, he added an oath. Basically, he was saying, "I swear by God that I do not know him." (Matthew 26:71-72). Again, Peter went down under the verbal attack of a servant girl. He called God as his witness, yet a short while ago he would not listen to God or obey him. He did not keep watch for God and did not pray to God. Yet he would use God to save his own skin. It was a terrible way to deny Jesus. Even now, he was relying on his own strength to get through this crisis. Peter had fallen, but not far enough to acknowledge his failings and for his pride to crumble.

Luke 22:58 says Peter's second denial came a little after his first, which took place at around 01:45 Hours. How long is, 'a little after'? A reasonable estimate for the amount of time that it took would be around fifteen minutes. If that is correct then Peter would have denied Jesus the second time at around 02:00 Hours.

02:00-03:00

02:00 Hours to 03:00 Hours

Jesus' trial by Caiaphas

After Annas questioned Jesus, he sent him to be tried by Caiaphas and the Sanhedrin. It was the religious and legal body that governed the Jewish people, even under Roman rule. The Sanhedrin consisted of seventy men plus the high priest, Caiaphas. It needed at least twenty-five members to be present to carry out its business lawfully and only during the hours of day. The members who gathered that night would have been those who had the same hatred of Jesus as Caiaphas and the same desire to have him killed. They would have been happy to have been woken in the middle of the night and break their own laws in order to fulfil their desire of having Jesus killed.

However, they had a problem. They had no legal charge against him. They brought in witnesses to testify against Jesus in order to find a charge against him. For that charge to stick, they needed the testimony of at least two witnesses to agree. They got many false witnesses to testify against Jesus, but their statements did not agree. Finally, they brought in two men who said they had heard Jesus say, '*I will destroy this temple made with human hands and build another in three days, not made with hands.*' But their testimonies did not agree. The religious leaders' hatred of Jesus was so great they were happy to break the Law to achieve their purposes – even paying men to falsely testify against him; '*you shall not bear false witness against your neighbour!*" (Exodus 20:16). They had rushed his arrest and trial and had not fully prepared their witnesses to get a conviction.

47

02:00 Hours to 03:00 Hours

Jesus said he was the Christ

The religious leaders had to produce concrete evidence against Jesus to sentence him to death, but his trial reached an impasse when none of their witnesses' testimonies agreed. To move things on and to get Jesus to incriminate himself, Caiaphas asked if he was going to answer any of the charges against him. Jesus ignored his questions and stayed silent (Matthew 26:59-63 and Mark 14:55-61).

Then Caiaphas made a final effort to draw an admission from Jesus that would be a cause for his condemnation. A confession he was the Son of God would result in a charge of blasphemy against him by the Sanhedrin. It would lay the foundation for a trial and death sentence for treason before the Roman authority in Israel. So Caiaphas went straight to the heart of the matter and asked the question in such a way that Jesus could not refuse to answer, "*I charge you before the living God, tell us if you are the Christ!*" He was asking Jesus to swear in God's name if he was the Christ, the Son of God. If he said no, they would have to dismiss him as innocent or start his trial all over again, which would mean bringing in more witnesses to testify against him.

However, Jesus could not be silent now in the face of this challenge to his identity and to his mission made by the official representative of his people, the Jews. Jesus gave Caiaphas and the Sanhedrin a clear and unequivocal answer that would leave no doubt about his teaching concerning his identity and his mission: "*You have said it,*" he told Caiaphas, "*and I tell you that you shall see the Son of Man sitting at the right hand of the Mighty One and coming on the clouds of heaven.*" (Matthew 26:63-64 and Mark 14:61-62). Before the leading religious figure of the Jewish people and the leading figures in the supreme court of Israel, God's chosen people, Jesus declared that he was the Christ, the Son of God, who is God. When he said this, Jesus made the greatest claim that this world has ever heard.

02:00 Hours to 03:00 Hours

He made this claim in the worst of circumstances; in the midst of false witnesses; trumped up charges and a blatant manipulation of power by those God had appointed to govern his people in righteousness and justice. However, Caiaphas was not listening. He had heard the words he wanted to hear: '*I am!*' He tore his robes and accused Jesus of blasphemy. The other Jewish religious leaders agreed and said it made Jesus worthy of death (Matthew 26:63-66 and Mark 14:61-64). When Jesus said he was the Son of God, who was God, the leaders of the Jewish people condemned him for blasphemy. None of them stopped to consider the enormity of their sin if what Jesus had said was true and their ensuing actions were wrong.

The verdict did not relieve the pent-up hatred the leaders had in their hearts for Jesus. It overflowed beyond all boundaries of decency and self-respect. Some of them spat in Jesus' face. This was a sign of supreme contempt in Bible times. Not content with spitting on Jesus, they and others began to strike him. They rained down blows on the Son of God from all sides. Some of the religious leaders slapped him and struck him with the back of their hands and others hit him with their fists. Next, they blindfolded Jesus and took turns to strike him then asked him to prophesy which of them had hit him (Mark 14:65).

Jesus accepted these slaps and blows and insults in silence. He did not react or protest or lash out as he drank the next mouthful of the cup his heavenly Father had set before him. He did all of this in loving obedience to his Father and out of his great love for us. His true status and dignity are revealed in the most degrading of circumstances. In his humiliation, his true identity is revealed. He is such a wonderfully humble and gracious Saviour. If Jesus' trial by Annas ended after 02:00 Hours; then his trial by Caiaphas and the Sanhedrin would have begun after that time. This trial would have continued up to and possibly past 03:00 Hours of the morning that Jesus Christ, the Son of God was crucified on the cross of Calvary.

02:00 Hours to 03:00 Hours

Peter's third denial

Peter denied Jesus the second time as he stood in the shadows near the gate to the courtyard of the high priest's palace. Luke 22:59 says an hour passed between his second and third denials. During that time, Peter moved from the gateway back to the fire. It seems Peter's anxiety about Jesus' fate outweighed his fears as he waited to see the outcome (Matthew 26:58). Twice Peter had been accused of being a disciple. If he thought his two rebuttals had been accepted and it was safe to remain there then he was totally wrong.

Standing by the fire enabled those standing nearby to see Peter's features more clearly. One man recognised him from the Garden of Gethsemane. Not only was Peter being accused of being a disciple of Jesus, he was being accused of being present at his arrest and being the one who had cut off the ear of the high priest's servant. It seems after his second denial, some in the courtyard had not let the matter go and had been discussing Peter's identity. They decided he was a disciple, because he was a Galilean. They knew that Jesus and his disciples were from Galilee. When Peter spoke with a Galilean accent they accused him for that reason. Peter's own mouth condemned him. His mouth set him up for a fall and his mouth brought it about.

Those standing there said to him, "*Surely you are one of them; your accent gives you away.*" Under pressure, a simple denial was no longer enough. He multiplied his denials and called down curses and swore to them, "*I don't know the man you're talking about!*" He was so wrapped up in himself he could not call Jesus by name. As soon as he said it a rooster crowed. Then Peter recalled Jesus' words to him: "*Before the rooster crows, you will disown me three times.*" At that very moment, Jesus turned and looked straight at Peter. It was such a look of love that it broke him and he went outside and wept bitterly (Matthew 26:73-75; Mark 14:70-72 and Luke 22:59-62).

02:00 Hours to 03:00 Hours

Whilst Jesus was being questioned by the high priest in his palace, Peter, his servant was questioned outside in the palace courtyard by the high priest's servants. Jesus was tried by leaders. Peter was tried by servants. Those questioning Jesus lied and manipulated the truth. Those questioning Peter wanted to know the truth of his relationship with Jesus. Jesus spoke the truth about himself and refused to deny his identity as the Son of God. Peter lied about himself and denied his identity as Jesus' disciple. Jesus was ready to take the consequence for speaking the truth and confessing his true identity even though it would lead to suffering and death inflicted by others. Peter was not prepared to face the consequences for speaking the truth and confessing his true identity. He lied with an oath to avoid suffering and death, but his denials did not protect him from suffering. After his third denial, he saw Jesus looking at him. Peter realised that he had fulfilled Jesus' words about denying him three times and he went outside and wept bitterly. Jesus' pain and suffering were inflicted by others. Peter's pain and suffering were self-inflicted.

Jesus was willing to lose his life in order to save others. Peter clung to his own life and risked losing everything that gave it meaning. Peter acted against his own deepest desires and the way he saw himself. In Gethsemane, Jesus had told Peter that his spirit was willing, but his flesh was weak. He had experienced that truth when he fell asleep three times after Jesus had asked him to watch and pray. Because he did not watch and pray in the garden, Peter lacked the power to get through this trial in the palace courtyard. Peter tried to deal with the accusations in his own strength and failed miserably. The only way Peter could have drawn on God's power was by acknowledging his vulnerabilities and knowing his weaknesses. Only God's power could have enabled Peter to overcome his natural tendency to save his own skin at the cost of what he believed and to be strong in his identity as a disciple of Jesus, regardless of the cost.

02:00 Hours to 03:00 Hours

Jesus trusted in the power of God, but Peter trusted in his own courage. Peter had to learn that he was weak, helpless and fallible. The power of God endures suffering and identifies itself with those who suffer. Peter stands for human weakness, which lacks self-knowledge and knowledge of God and the power of God and the power of prayer to tap into the power of God. Peter' suffering was self-inflicted and it achieved nothing for others. Jesus' suffering was God ordained and it achieved everything on behalf of sinful mankind.

The third accusation that Peter was a disciple came about because of his accent. It was his mouth that got him into trouble. It was his mouth that started the trouble when he boasted he would never leave Jesus or deny him and his mouth got him into trouble when he denied Jesus in the courtyard. His mouth spoke from the overflow of pride in his heart. He spoke with a Galilean accent to people from Jerusalem. It was his mouth that committed the greatest sin that night – denying Jesus three times. In his pride, Peter made a fool of himself. He proved he had lied when he said he would never deny Jesus. He lied about knowing him and was prepared to use anyone, even God to get himself out of trouble. Peter fell a long way and in God's eyes he needed to. God allowed him to fall, because with his pride and self-reliance intact, he could not serve well in the kingdom of God.

Despite being in the courtyard with all of Jesus' enemies, the biggest danger to Peter that night was himself and God saw this. When it all appeared hopeless, God intervened to save Peter from himself and brought him back to himself. However, it was not through angels or heavenly messengers or through a trumpet call. It was through the simple crow of a rooster. It was the crow of a rooster that marked the end of Peter's fall. As soon as he heard it, Peter recalled Jesus' words, *"before the rooster crows, you will disown me three times."* Jesus had given him a prophecy with a clear audible signal. When Peter heard that signal, he realised that he had fulfilled Jesus' words.

02:00 Hours to 03:00 Hours

After Peter had denied Jesus the third time and the rooster crowed, he looked in the Lord's direction only to see Jesus staring back at him. However, it was not a condemnatory look. It was a look of pure love. The one Peter had hurt the most by his denials was looking right at him in total love. Despite all of his boasting, all of his lies, all of his oaths and all of his cursing, Jesus still absolutely loved Peter. He may have denied Jesus, but he was not denying Peter. It was such a look of love that it broke Peter's heart and he went outside and wept.

In brokenness and humility and his strength spent, Peter went and repented. With his pride in tatters and his face in the dirt, he wept. Peter ended the night in the same place where Jesus had started his – on his knees, weeping and crying out to God. If Peter had started the night on his knees in prayer then he would not have ended it on his knees weeping uncontrollably. In humility, he knelt before God broken. In broken-heartedness, he wept before God. It was only in that condition that he could be useful to God in the kingdom of God. It was only in that level of humility and brokenness he could lead the Church of Jesus. It was a truth he learned after the Resurrection.

When roosters crow in Jerusalem

Peter denied Jesus the third time as the rooster crowed. If we can establish the time roosters crow, it will reveal the time of Peter's third denial. Mark 13:35 says as Jesus taught his disciples about his return, he said, "*Keep watch, as you do not know when the owner of the house will return, whether in the evening, or at midnight or **when the rooster crows** or at dawn.*" Jesus divided night into four parts:

Four parts of night

1.) Evening
2.) Midnight
3.) When roosters crow
4.) Dawn

02:00 Hours to 03:00 Hours

The hours of night begin when evening falls at sunset and they end at dawn at sunrise. The annual average time the sun sets in Israel is 18:00 Hours and the annual average time of sunrises is 06:00 Hours. 24:00 Hours (midnight) is the midpoint between evening and dawn. It is the same division of night Jesus used in Mark 13:35. If he used the same division of time between midnight (24:00 Hours) and dawn (06:00 Hours) for the time that roosters crow then they must crow at 03:00 Hours. That would mean that Peter would have denied Jesus for the third time around 03:00 Hours. Luke 22:59 says Peter's third denial happened about an hour after his second denial. That would mean that Peter denied Jesus the second time around 02:00 Hours.

Luke 22:58 says that Peter's second denial took place a little after his first denial. If there was only about fifteen minutes between those two denials and Peter's second denial occurred around 02:00 Hours then his first denial would have happened around 01:45 Hours. John 18:19 says Peter's first denial took place at the same time as Jesus was being tried by Annas and that trial began at 01:45 Hours. It was after Jesus' trial by Annas ended that Peter denied him the second time. If that denial happened around 02:00 Hours then his trial by Annas ended about that time. Jesus was sent to be tried by Caiaphas after his trial by Annas, so his trial before the high priest and the Sanhedrin would have begun around 02:00 Hours.

At his trial by Caiaphas, Jesus was condemned for blasphemy. Then the leaders spat on him and beat him before placing him under guard. Luke 22:61 says as Peter denied Jesus the third time, the Lord looked straight at him. If this happened as Jesus was being led away by the guards following his trial by Caiaphas then that trial would have ended around 03:00 Hours. If Jesus was still being tried by Caiaphas when he looked down at Peter in the courtyard of the high priest's palace then his trial by the Sanhedrin would have finished after 03:00 Hours.

03:00-04:00

03:00 Hours to 04:00 Hours

Jesus was kept under guard

After the leaders had beaten Jesus, he was kept under guard until he was sentenced by the Sanhedrin at dawn. The men guarding Jesus mocked and beat him. They blindfolded him, hit him then demanded, *"Prophesy! Who hit you?"* And they said many other insulting things to him (Mark 14:65 and Luke 22:63-66). Jesus was repeatedly hit with fists, slapped, beaten and mocked, yet he offered no resistance, self-defence or retaliation during his suffering. In all this we see the total perfection and maturity of Jesus. He had no pride, no hatred, no self-pity, no thought for himself. When the guards tired of beating Jesus, he was locked up like a common criminal. He could have used his position as the Son of God to escape his ordeal at any point, but he chose not to. Jesus chose to see his ordeal through at every point – right until the end. Only by seeing it through to the end could Jesus redeem us from our sins. He spent that night alone in the hands of the guards. Jesus was alone, humanly speaking, but God was with him.

If the trial by Caiaphas and the Sanhedrin ended shortly before or shortly after Peter denied Jesus for the third time at 03:00 Hours then the Son of God would have been kept under guard from that time until the religious leaders met at dawn to condemn him. The solar calendar for Jerusalem says the sun rises in the current year at Passover at 05:50 Hours[a]. If it breaks at that time nowadays, it would have broken at 05:50 Hours on the day Jesus was crucified. The Son of God would have been imprisoned from 03:00 Hours to 05:50 Hours and he would have spent the period, 03:00 Hours to 04:00 Hours under guard.

03:00 Hours to 04:00 Hours

Jesus, the innocent Son of God was locked up like a common criminal. There has never been a greater miscarriage of justice than Jesus' trials, sentencing and crucifixion. It was all part of God's will that His sinless Son died for our sins and the sins of the world on the cross of Calvary. Because of all Jesus went through, he can draw alongside us and comfort us in our times of need. Jesus knows what it is like to be imprisoned. From his own experience he can comfort, sympathise and help all who have been and who are imprisoned unjustly (and there are many). But it is not just those who are imprisoned behind bars that Jesus draws alongside. Because of what he suffered in the time before and during his crucifixion, he is able to help those who are imprisoned in the physical, the mental, the emotional and the spiritual as well as those imprisoned by the cruelty of others. What a wonderful Saviour and friend we have in Jesus.

04:00-05:00

04:00 Hours to 05:00 Hours

Jesus was kept under guard

After the religious leaders had spat on him, blindfolded him and beaten him with their fists, they handed him over to their guards. The men who guarded him took him and began to beat him and mock him. They blindfolded Jesus and demanded that he prophesy and tell them who had hit him. Then they said many other insulting things to him. Jesus was kept under guard until he was tried by the Sanhedrin when they met at dawn (Mark 14:65 and Luke 22:63-66).

Jesus could have used his position as God's Son to escape, but he did not. He chose to stay and suffer the beatings, insults and mockery at the hands of those ignorant guards. When they had tired of striking Jesus, he was led to a cell and locked up like a common criminal. He was alone in that cell. Yet this was not the first time and it would not be the last time that he was alone during his Passion.

Jesus was alone in the Garden of Gethsemane. His disciples were supposed to be with him and watch over him, but they fell asleep. Jesus was alone in his trials. All the leaders were accusing him, but no one stood alongside Jesus to defend him. He was alone in his cell. He was alone physically in all these circumstances. Yet he was not alone. His Father was with him. In the garden, when he submitted his will and his all to his Father, he ensured his Father was with him. God even sent an angel, a heavenly messenger to strengthen His Son as he prayed. Jesus showed it is vital to keep the lines of communication open with our heavenly Father even when things are at their worst.

04:00 Hours to 05:00 Hours

Jesus left us an example of what to do when we are struggling to obey and when we are wrestling with temptation. Jesus who is the way – showed us the way. His disciples did not follow his way and so when temptation came – when things were at their worst, they tried to deal with it in their own strength and their own wit and forfeited God's strength that was freely available to them to be victorious in their trials. As a result, they failed miserably. What was true for Jesus and his disciples is true for us today. We can watch and pray and draw on God's resources in times of trial or we can sleepwalk through life and try to deal with life's trials in our own strength and resources. If we do, then like Peter and the other disciples, we will fail in times of testing.

God always gives us the choice to follow His way or to follow our own way. Also, He has been gracious to us to give us examples in His Word – the Bible of the consequences of each choice. If we follow Jesus' example, we will have the strength and the wherewithal to face even death. If we follow Peter and the disciples' example, we will fail when temptations and times of crises come in our lives.

If the trial by Caiaphas ended shortly before or shortly after Peter's third denial at 03:00 Hours, Jesus would have been kept under guard from then until dawn. The solar calendar for Jerusalem says the sun rises at 05:50 Hours[a] at the time of the Passover in the current year. If dawn breaks at that time nowadays in Israel, then it would have broken at 05:50 Hours on the day that Jesus died. Jesus would have been imprisoned from 03:00 Hours to 05:50 Hours and he would have spent the period, 04:00 Hours to 05:00 Hours under guard.

05:00-06:00

05:00 Hours to 06:00 Hours

Jesus was kept under guard

After the religious leaders had spat on him, blindfolded him and beaten him with their fists, Jesus was kept under guard until he was tried by the Sanhedrin at daybreak. The men who were guarding him began mocking him and beating him. Then they blindfolded him and demanded, *"Prophesy! Who hit you?"* And they said many other insulting things to him (Mark 14:65 and Luke 22:63-65). If the trial by Caiaphas ended shortly before or shortly after Peter's third denial at 03:00 Hours, Jesus would have been kept under guard from then until daybreak. Daybreak is dawn or sunrise. The Jerusalem solar calendar says that the sun rises in the current year at the time of Passover at 05:50 Hours[a]. If it breaks at that time nowadays, it would have broken at 05:50 Hours on the day the Son of God was crucified. Jesus would have been imprisoned from 03:00 Hours to 05:50 Hours and he would have spent the period, 05:00 Hours to 05:50 Hours under guard.

Jesus spent the night in the hands of the guards. He was alone. Only God was with him. He could have used his position as the Son of God to escape, but he did not. He chose to stay and suffer the beatings, insults and mockery of the ignorant guards. When they had tired of striking Jesus, he was led to a cell and locked up like a common criminal. Jesus was repeatedly hit with fists, slapped, beaten and mocked, yet he offered no resistance, self-defence or retaliation. In all this we see the absolute perfection and maturity of Jesus. He had no pride, hatred, self-pity and no thought for himself.

05:00 Hours to 06:00 Hours

Jesus was condemned

It seems the Sanhedrin met at dawn to sentence Jesus. According to the Jewish law, there had to be twenty-four hours between a person being convicted and sentenced. However, Jesus was not concerned about the illegality of his trial and the humiliation of it all. He was focused on seeing his Father's will being done. The leaders asked the question he had answered earlier that had led to his conviction, *"Are you the Christ?"* He said, *"If I tell you, you will not believe. If I question you, you will not answer me or let me go."* (Luke 22:66-68). He was telling them that they were not really searching for the truth. They had no intention of believing him despite all of his teachings that they had heard and his miracles that they had seen. Nor would they answer his questions about his true identity and his God-given role as Christ.

To them, Jesus was a fraud and a blasphemer and was worthy of death. When he said, *"It is just as you say, I am!"* the leaders had the evidence they needed to accuse him of blasphemy and sentence him to death. As they had no authority to execute anyone, they took him to Pilate the Roman governor, who could condemn and crucify him. If they had killed Jesus, it would have been by stoning, the penalty for blasphemy. It was a horrible way to die, but it came nowhere near to the type of death God needed his Son to die to pay for the sins of the world. Sin is hideous and a hideous price had to be paid for it. It was this type of death Jesus had consented to, to pay for our sins.

The priests, religious leaders and the members of the Sanhedrin met at daybreak to condemn Jesus. Dawn broke that day at 05:50 Hours. It would not have taken them long to condemn Jesus. If it took more than ten minutes to condemn him then this trial by Caiaphas and the Sanhedrin would have begun at 05:50 Hours and it would have continued past 06:00 Hours on the day that Jesus died.

06:00-07:00

06:00 Hours to 07:00 Hours

Jesus was taken to Pontius Pilate

To the religious leaders, Jesus' claim that he was the Christ, the Son of God was blasphemous. In their eyes the penalty for the crime was death, but they had no authority to execute anyone as Israel was under the rule of the Roman Empire. They needed the consent of its governor in Israel, Pontius Pilate. So, after the priests and elders had condemned Jesus, they led him off to Pilate (Matthew 27:1-2).

Jesus would have been bound, led from his cell into the courtyard of the high priest's palace and an escort would have formed around him. The group would have exited the main gate into Jerusalem's narrow streets and headed east for a short time before turning north. The cobbled streets descended into the Tyropean Valley that cut the city in two. After crossing the valley, they would have ascended the streets to Pilate's fortress, situated on the hill, north of the temple.

The group would have entered the Antonia Fortress via the Western gate and waited in the courtyard for Pilate to come out and speak to them. They refused to enter his (a gentile's) palace as it would make them unclean and they would be unable to attend the Passover Feast. The walk there would have taken about thirty minutes[13]. The leaders met to condemn Jesus at dawn. Dawn broke that day at 05:50 Hours. If it took Caiaphas and the Sanhedrin over ten minutes to condemn Jesus then the journey from the high priest's palace would have begun after 06:00 Hours. The half-hour journey would have seen them arrive at Pilate's Antonia Fortress after 06:30 Hours.

06:00 Hours to 07:00 Hours

Judas Iscariot killed himself

When Judas saw that Jesus had been condemned, he was filled with remorse. He went to the temple to return the silver the priests had paid him to betray Jesus, saying he had sinned by betraying innocent blood. When they said it was his responsibility not theirs, he threw the thirty coins into the temple then killed himself. The priests said, *"It is against the law to put this into the treasury as it is blood money."* They used it to buy the potter's field as a burial place for foreigners. It was called the Field of Blood. It fulfilled the words of Zechariah 11:12-13: *"'They took the thirty pieces of silver, the price set on me by the people of Israel, and used them to buy the potter's field, as the Lord commanded me.'"* (Matthew 27:1-10).

Judas may have discovered Jesus had been condemned when he saw the religious leaders marching him off to Pilate at 06:00 Hours. Judas would have returned the money to the priests and hanged himself after that time. Matthew 27:11 says he returned the coins at the same time, *'as Jesus stood before the governor.'* If Jesus arrived at Pilate's Antonia Fortress after 06:30 Hours then the events of Judas' death began at 06:00 hours and ended after 06:30 Hours.

Judas' reaction after he saw Jesus was condemned was remorse. It is not the same as repentance. He was concerned about what he had done and was angry with himself. He sought a human solution by returning the money he got for betraying Jesus. Then he tried to wipe out his sin by paying the price with his own life. If he had waited a few hours, Jesus paid the price for his sin with his life. After denying Jesus three times, Peter wept bitterly in true repentance. He was forgiven, lifted up and restored. After his resurrection, Jesus restored Peter to his ministry, filled him with the Spirit and made him the head of his Church. If Judas had truly repented and not tried to make amends himself, he too would have been forgiven.

06:00 Hours to 07:00 Hours

Jesus' trial by Pilate

After the leaders arrived at Pilate's fortress after 06:30 Hours, he asked what charges they were bringing against Jesus. When they said if he was not a criminal they would not have handed him over to him, he told them to go and judge him by their laws. The leaders showed their true intentions when they told Pilate they had no right to execute anyone. Then they accused Jesus of subverting their nation, opposing paying taxes to Caesar and claiming to be a king.

Pilate was amazed when Jesus gave no reply to their accusations. He asked, *"Don't you hear the testimony they are bringing against you?"* When he stayed silent, he asked, *"Are you the king of the Jews?"* *"Is that your idea,"* Jesus asked, *"or did others talk to you about me?"* *"Am I a Jew?"* Pilate replied, *"Your people and chief priests handed you over to me. What is it you have done?"* Jesus said, *"My kingdom is not of this world. If it were, my servants would fight to prevent my arrest by the Jews. My kingdom is from another place."* *"You are a king, then!"* said Pilate. He replied, *"You are right in saying I am a king. The reason I was born and came into the world is to testify to the truth. Everyone on the side of truth listens to me."* *"What is truth?"* Pilate asked. Then he told the leaders, *"I find no basis for a charge against this man."* (Matthew 27:11-14 and John 18:29-38).

They had hoped their charges against Jesus would persuade Pilate to sentence him to death. They failed to see their hypocrisy. After arriving at his fortress, in a show of piety, they refused to defile themselves by entering his palace so they could celebrate Passover. Yet they had no qualms about seeking the death of the pure Lamb of God, whose blood would cleanse all sin (even theirs). Their concern about outward cleanliness and Passover rituals prevented them seeing the fulfilment of the Passover – God's Passover Lamb standing right in front of them.

06:00 Hours to 07:00 Hours

The trumped-up charges they presented to Pilate against Jesus were mixed with lies and hypocrisy. He was not a political revolutionary threatening Rome's government. Jesus had never said paying taxes to Caesar was illegal, but told the people to give to Caesar what was Caesar's and to give to God what was God's. He never claimed to be king of a worldly kingdom. Being a bad religious influence and not paying taxes was not going to convince Pilate to execute him as most Jews did not or tried not to pay taxes to Caesar. It was only when they claimed Jesus was a king that Pilate was interested.

Jesus' trial by the Sanhedrin focussed on theological issues about the temple and blasphemy. Jesus' trial by Pilate focussed on political issues – whether he was king of the Jews. His kingship had as many theological implications for the leaders as it had political ones for Rome. Both trials emphasise Jesus, the ruler of the universe's powerlessness before the civil and religious authorities of his day on Earth. They all abused their power against he who is all-powerful.

Pilate did not care if Jesus was a king; he just wanted to know out of curiosity. But he was aware Jesus had done something terrible to so upset the Jewish leaders that they were willing to hand him over to a non-Jew to be killed at Passover. However, Jesus reassured Pilate he was no threat to Rome. If he had been, he would have called his army to prevent his arrest by the Jews. He did not have an army, because his kingdom was not of this world. Then he told Pilate he was the king of truth – that is, the God of reality. According to God's truth – truth can only be found in the person of Jesus Christ.

After questioning Jesus, Pilate was convinced he was no threat to Rome. He went and told the Jewish leaders he found Jesus innocent. If Jesus arrived at Pilate's fortress around 06:30 Hours after the half-hour walk from the high priest's palace then his trial by Pilate began at that time and it would have continued past 07:00 Hours.

07:00-08:00

07:00 Hours to 08:00 Hours

Jesus' trial by Herod

After Pilate said he could find no basis for a charge against Jesus, the leaders insisted he had stirred people up, all over Israel, starting in Galilee before coming to Jerusalem (Luke 23:4-5). When he learned Jesus was from Galilee, Pilate realised it placed him under King Herod's jurisdiction. The tetrarch of Galilee was in Jerusalem at that time for the Passover Feast, so he sent Jesus to be tried by him. Herod would have stayed at his Hasmonean palace. It was about four hundred yards from Pilate's fortress. It was built on the west hill of the city, high above the Tyropean Valley. Its walls and windows looked down into the temple area across the valley to the east.

Pilate would have sent an official message to Herod to tell him what was taking place. Jesus would have been surrounded by soldiers and led out of the fortress, followed by the Jewish leaders. The group would have headed south down the cobbled streets to the Tyropean Valley. After crossing the valley, they would have turned west and climbed the hill to Herod's palace. The walk from Pilate's Antonia fortress would have taken about twenty minutes[14]. Herod was pleased to see Jesus as for a long time he had wanted to see him. From what he had heard about Jesus, he hoped to see him perform a miracle. Herod plied him with many questions, but Jesus gave him no answers. The religious leaders vehemently accused him, but he stayed silent. When Herod saw Jesus was not going to respond to his questions or the leaders' accusations or perform any miracles, he and his soldiers ridiculed and mocked him (Luke 23:7-12).

07:00 Hours to 08:00 Hours

Herod Antipas may not have known much about Jesus, but the Lord knew a lot about him as there was a historical legacy between them. About thirty years earlier his father, King Herod the Great had tried to kill Jesus when he learned that the king of the Jews had been born in Bethlehem. He ordered all male babies under the age of two who had been born in that town to be killed (Matthew 2:1-18). Herod Antipas himself may have not realised that when he jailed and beheaded John the Baptist, he had executed Jesus' cousin (Mark 6:14-28).

When Herod met Jesus, he wanted him to entertain him and his court soldiers, like a performer doing a magic show. Despite his pressing questions and the vehement accusations made against him by the Jewish religious leaders, Jesus stood in quiet dignity. It would have been Jesus' silence that made the situation a little awkward for Herod. It provoked him and his soldiers to mock him. After he had got some form of cheap entertainment from Jesus, he dressed him in a purple robe then sent him back to Pilate. Pilate had sent him a man claiming to be the king of the Jews, so he sent him back dressed like a king.

Jesus would have been marched out of the Great Hall, across the courtyard and into the street. Surrounded by soldiers and religious leaders, he would have been led down the steep hill to the Tyropean Valley. After crossing the valley, the group would have walked for a few hundred yards along the other side before climbing the slope and heading north to Pilate's Antonia Fortress. The walk from Herod's palace would have taken around twenty minutes[15] at the most. The journeys to and from the Hasmonean palace and Jesus' trial by Herod would probably have taken less than an hour. It would have happened from 07:00 Hours to 08:00 Hours on the day that Jesus died.

08:00-09:00

08:00 Hours to 09:00 Hours

Jesus was condemned to die

After Jesus' trial by Herod, Pilate told the chief priests, elders and the people, "*You brought me this man as one who incites the people to rebellion. I have examined him in your presence and have found no basis for your charges against him. Nor has Herod for he sent him back to us; as you can see, he has done nothing to deserve death. So, I will punish him and release him*" (Luke 23:13-16).

Throughout the trials, Pilate had passed the buck, but it kept coming back to him. First, he told the Jewish leaders to try him themselves, but they were having none of it. When Pilate learned that Jesus was a Galilean, he passed the buck a second time and sent him to be tried by Herod, the ruler of Galilee hoping he would decide for him, but that did not happen. Pilate knew Jesus was innocent, but if he did not condemn him, the religious leaders would report him to the Emperor for releasing a man who claimed to be a king. Any king was a threat in the eyes of Rome. To get out of this dilemma, Pilate passed the buck again, this time to the crowd gathered before him. The crowd expected Pilate to fulfil his usual custom at Passover of releasing a prisoner to the people. Pilate put Jesus forward as one of the two prisoners to be released. He believed the crowd would choose Jesus rather than Barabbas who was a well-known insurrectionist and murderer. However, Pilate's plan to get Jesus released failed when the Jewish religious leaders stirred up the crowd to call for Barabbas to be released and for Jesus to be condemned.

08:00 Hours to 09:00 Hours

Pilate was the only champion Jesus had during this ordeal, but he was a weak champion. Determined to have Jesus released, he adopted another strategy and had him flogged. He hoped it would satisfy the crowd that he had been punished enough and they would no longer seek his death. He knew Jesus was innocent and saw through the leaders' accusations. His wife confirmed his unease by telling him not to have anything to do with this innocent man as she had suffered greatly in a dream due to Jesus (Matthew 27:19). However, Pilate was too weak to see justice done.

When Pilate sent Jesus to be flogged, he would have been stripped and tied to a post. He was whipped with leather thongs full of bits of lead and jagged bone, which would have dug into his skin and tore it open as the whip was pulled back. His chest, shoulders, neck, back, hips and legs would have been slashed as with knives, streaked with blue welts and swollen bruises. His flesh would have been exposed over many parts and his face disfigured by the lashes rained on him. Jesus would have been a pitiable sight after his flogging and would have been almost unrecognisable. Though he was wearing a purple robe – he looked nothing like a king. Pilate rightly said, "*Here is the man! Here is your king!*" In his eyes Jesus had been punished enough and should be let go. He believed the crowd would agree.

When he asked the crowd, "*Which of the two do you want me to release to you?*" the Jewish religious leaders persuaded the people to ask for Barabbas, a notorious criminal to be freed. Then Pilate asked them what he should do with Jesus, the Christ. They cried, "*Crucify him!*" When he asked them why and what crime he had committed, they shouted all the louder, "*Crucify him!*" So another plan by Pilate to have Jesus released had failed. However, throughout this ordeal, Jesus stood and bore it all in silent, patient dignity. He knew that his suffering was part of his Father's plan for the salvation of all who would repent and believe he is Christ, the Son of God, who is God.

08:00 Hours to 09:00 Hours

When the crowd continued to shout for Jesus' crucifixion, Pilate told the religious leaders, *"You take him and crucify him. As for me, I find no basis for a charge against him."* Pilate was challenging them to respect his laws, but they challenged him to respect theirs. They told him, *"We have a law and according to that law he must die, for he claimed to be the Son of God."* Already, Pilate had dealt with Jesus' claim that he was a king, now he had to deal with the claim that the innocent man standing before him was God. It took things to another level and Pilate became even more afraid. He asked Jesus, *"Where do you come from?"* But he gave the Roman governor no answer.

Pilate asked him *"Do you refuse to speak to me? Don't you realise I have power either to free you or crucify you?"* Jesus said, *"You would have no power over me if it were not given to you from above".* Pilate had authority over him, because God had given it to him. Pilate was not in control – God was. Jesus reaffirmed his certainty that he was in God's care and not at Pilate's mercy. When Jesus said, *"The one who handed me over to you is guilty of a greater sin,"* he was saying it was not Pilate, but the Jewish religious leaders who had committed the greater sin when they offered Jesus up to be killed. Pilate responded to this kindness. He tried to get him released and turned to the crowd again. He asked them whether they wanted him to release Jesus.

They shouted, *"If you let this man go, you are no friend of Caesar. Anyone claiming to be a king opposes Caesar."* When Pilate heard this, he said, *"Here is your king."* But they shouted, *"Take him away! Crucify him!"* *"Shall I crucify your king?"* He asked. *"We have no king but Caesar,"* the leaders answered. When Pilate saw he was getting nowhere and an uproar was starting, he washed his hands and said, *"I am innocent of this man's blood. It is your responsibility!"* All the people answered, *"Let his blood be on us and on our children!"* So he released Barabbas to the crowd then handed Jesus over to be crucified (Matthew 27:15-26; Luke 23:13-25 and John 18:38-19:16).

08:00 Hours to 09:00 Hours

Barabbas, the taker of life was freed and Jesus, the giver of life was condemned. The religious leaders had rejected Jesus, God's Christ out of hypocrisy, envy and unbelief and treated him contemptuously and cruelly. Mark 15:25 says Jesus was crucified at the third Hebrew hour, which is 09:00 Hours in Western time. If the walk from Pilate's fortress to Calvary took half an hour (see below); Pilate would have handed him over to the soldiers to be crucified before 08:30 Hours.

Soldiers took charge of Jesus

The soldiers took Jesus into the Praetorium. They gathered around him the whole company of soldiers and mocked him for the crime for which he had been condemned – sedition. They ripped off his blood-soaked robe that was matted to his flesh, exposed by his flogging. The pain would have been intolerable. They dressed him in a purple robe then made a crown of thorns and fixed it on Jesus' head. The needle-like thorns would have pierced his scalp, causing severe pain. They put a staff in his hand then hit him repeatedly on the head with it. The blows would have bruised him and caused swelling and would have driven the crown of thorns deeper into his scalp, causing Jesus even more pain. Then the soldiers fell on their knees before him and mockingly paid homage to Jesus. They called out to him, "*Hail, king of the Jews!*" Some of the soldiers spat on him and others took the staff and struck Jesus on the head again and again.

Jesus suffered it all in silence. He was revealed as king in the most appalling of circumstances as he was beaten and mocked. Ironically, it is true. Jesus is a king, but not just any king. He is the King of kings and the Lord of lords. After mocking Jesus, the soldiers took off their robe and put his own clothes on him. Then they led him away to crucify him (Matthew 27:27-31 and Mark 15:16-20). If Jesus was crucified at 09:00 Hours (Mark 15:25) and it took half an hour to walk from Pilate's Antonia Fortress to Calvary (see below) then the soldiers would have mocked and beaten Jesus before 08:30 Hours.

08:00 Hours to 09:00 Hours

Journey to Calvary

Jesus was led out to Calvary with two robbers carrying their crosses. Roman Soldiers would have cleared the way followed by the centurion in charge of all the crucifixions, riding on his horse. Jesus and the two criminals with him followed, each surrounded by four soldiers who were in charge of their crucifixions. More soldiers brought up the rear. Crucifixions were held outside Jerusalem on a main road leading in and out of the city, where the victims could be easily seen by all who passed by. The soldiers would have made a display of their victims by leading them along a route through Jerusalem to be seen by as many people as possible. After exiting Pilate's fortress, they would have turned right and walked through the narrow streets of the city to the Tyropean Valley that split the capital in two. After crossing the valley, they would have headed in the direction of the Ephraim Gate.

It would have been slow going through the heavily populated area filled with crowds there to celebrate Passover. After navigating the incline to the Ephraim Gate, located where the north-south wall met the east-west wall, they would have exited the city along the road leading northwest to Jaffa. An elevated spot would have been found along the road to crucify them where all who passed by could see. It would have taken about half an hour to get to Calvary[16]. If Jesus was crucified at 09:00 Hours then this journey began about 08:30 Hours.

Simon carried Jesus' cross

Jesus' beatings and flogging would have weakened him to such an extent that he was unable to carry his cross all the way to Calvary. It may have been on the incline up to the Ephraim Gate when Jesus could no longer carry his cross. As Simon of Cyrene passed by on his way into the city from the countryside, the soldiers stopped him and forced him to carry Jesus' cross (Mark 15:21). Simon of Cyrene would have carried Jesus' cross from 08:30 Hours to 09:00 Hours.

08:00 Hours to 09:00 Hours

A crowd mourned for Jesus

As Jesus made his way to Calvary from 08:30 Hours to 09:00 Hours, a group of women followed, mourning for him. Jesus turned and told them not to mourn for him, but for themselves. He added that if men behaved this way when the tree was green, what would they do when the tree was dry (Luke 23:27-31). It would have been after his cross had been placed on Simon that Jesus could turn to address them. Jesus forgot about his own sufferings to warn the daughters of Jerusalem of the evils that would befall their city. Jesus was referring to the fall of Jerusalem to the Romans, which would happen in 70AD, just forty years after his death on the cross.

09:00 Hours

09:00 Hours

Jesus was crucified

They came to a place called Golgotha, which means, 'the place of the skull'. Then they offered Jesus wine mixed with gall and myrrh, but after tasting it, he refused to drink it. This concoction is generally understood to be a narcotic to help deaden the pain of crucifixion. Jesus refused to drink it, because he was going to suffer the full pain of his crucifixion totally conscious and with a clear mind. Then they crucified Jesus with the two criminals, who had been led out with him to Calvary, one on his right, the other on his left and he in the middle (Luke 23:33 and John 19:18). It fulfilled the prophecy in Isaiah 53:12: *'he was numbered with the transgressors.'* Also, it shows no matter what we have done or how low we fall in life, Jesus Christ, God's Son, who was numbered with the transgressors went lower than us to save and redeem us. We can never sink so low that we are beyond his redemption. That is how wonderful Jesus our Saviour is.

If earthly justice had been served that day, Barabbas would have hung on the cross, not Jesus. His crimes were worse than those of the two thieves and he deserved to hang in the prime position between them. Yet Barabbas was set free and Jesus was crucified. Jesus got what Barabbas deserved – crucifixion and Barabbas got what Jesus deserved – freedom. The cross reveals the innocent died for the guilty and the sinless died for sinners. The link between Jesus and Barabbas is a picture for us. As guilty sinners, we should have died for our sins, but God in His love for us let His pure, innocent Son pay the price for them all: past, present and future, and we go free.

09:00 Hours

Out of his love for his Father and for us, God's Son, Jesus submitted himself to death by crucifixion. The innocent Son of God chose to die in our place that we, the sinners might go free. This is the wonder of the cross – the wonder of Jesus' loving, selfless sacrifice. Jesus paid the price and we go free. It is too unbelievable to make up and too sublime for the human mind to comprehend. It is the revelation of God in the human heart that enables us to see that God himself died on the cross of Calvary for our sins. What wisdom! What love! What grace! What mercy! What a wonderful God we have in Jesus Christ!

Jesus, the Son of God, God himself, left heaven's splendour to come down to planet Earth to live among us. Jesus came to live among sinners and to live for sinners. He did not come to live for sinners only. He came to die for sinners as well. He came down to be among the lost; the sick; the diseased; the outcast; the disabled; the oppressed; the prisoners; the weak; the rejected; the failures; and the dying. He came for sinners. As all have sinned, he came for all of us. It does not matter how far we have fallen or how much we have failed. It does not matter how lost we are or how sick we are. Jesus came for all of us – each and every one of us. Jesus lived for sinners like us. He died for sinners like us and he rose to life for sinners like us. What a wonderful Saviour we have in Jesus Christ, the Son of God, who is God.

Jesus was born into this world to die for all of the sins of mankind. Now the time had come. Evil men crucified Jesus in the middle of two criminals to discredit him and shame him. However, God allowed it to show the world Jesus is the centre of all things. Jesus was the centre of creation, *'all things were made by him and through him'* (John 1:3). He is the centre between God and man. Jesus is the only way to God (John 14:6). Only through Jesus can sinful man be reconciled to God or be in relationship with God. Jesus was central in his ministry. He was always at the centre of the crowds. His disciples always gathered around him. And even when he died, Jesus was at the centre.

09:00 Hours

Jesus wants to be at the centre of our lives

After Jesus rose from the dead on the third day, he came and stood in the midst of his disciples in the Upper Room (Luke 24:36). After Jesus, the Lamb of God who died for the sins of the world ascended into heaven, the disciple John saw him, as the lamb who was slain, standing in the centre of heaven's throne. His kingly throne is at the centre of heaven, surrounded by the four living creatures, twenty-four elders and all the heavenly hosts (Revelation 5:6-11). In both his life and in his death and even in his resurrected form in heaven, Jesus, the Son of God was and is always at the centre of all things.

Jesus wants his life, death, resurrection and ascension into heaven to be at the centre of our lives. He himself wants to be at the centre of every aspect of our lives. He wants to be at the centre of our faith, the centre of our relationships, the centre of our families, the centre of our marriages, the centre of our work, the centre of our studies and the centre of our friendships. Jesus Christ, the Son of God, who died on the cross of Calvary for our sins and the world's sins, who was buried and rose on the third day and ascended into heaven, where he now sits at the right hand of God the Father, wants to be at the centre of all that we are, all that we have and all that we do. Jesus reigns over all things and when he is the centre of our lives and over all that we have and do then we reign over all things with him. What a Saviour!

Jesus was crucified at the third hour

Mark 15:25 says it was the third hour of the Hebrew Day when the Roman soldiers crucified Jesus. In Bible times, the Hebrew day was divided into twelve hourly segments that began at sunrise and ended at sunset. The average time that the sun rises in Israel throughout the year is 06:00 Hours and the average time it sets is 18:00 Hours. So the first hour in Israel would have begun at 06:00 Hours and the twelfth hour would have ended at 18:00 Hours, as shown below:

Western Hour   Hebrew Hour

06:00-07:00 Hours = First Hour
07:00-08:00 Hours = Second Hour
<u>08:00-09:00 Hours = Third Hour</u>
09:00-10:00 Hours = Fourth Hour
10:00-11:00 Hours = Fifth Hour
11:00-12:00 Hours = Sixth Hour
12:00-13:00 Hours = Seventh Hour
13:00-14:00 Hours = Eighth Hour
14:00-15:00 Hours = Ninth Hour
15:00-16:00 Hours = Tenth Hour
16:00-17:00 Hours = Eleventh Hour
17:00-18:00 Hours = Twelfth Hour

So the third hour in the Hebrew Day is 09:00 Hours in western time. Jesus Christ, the Son of God, who is God would have been nailed to the cross of Calvary for the sins of the world at 09:00 Hours.

09:00-10:00

09:00 Hours to 10:00 Hours

Jesus forgave his killers

Luke 23:33-34 says when they crucified Jesus he asked his Father to forgive his killers as they did not know what they were doing. They would have been the first words he uttered on the cross and his first words were to his Father, on behalf of his killers. During his ministry, his Father was always the first one Jesus turned to and it was his Father he turned to as he died in excruciating pain. Yet Jesus did not turn to his Father for himself. There was no sense of self-pity in him as he fulfilled his God-given destiny – to die for sinners on the cross. Despite the pain, he turned to his Father on behalf of those crucifying him – not to condemn them, but to forgive them. These men did their best to hammer the life out of Jesus, but they could not hammer the love out of him. He still loved and believed in his Father, despite the evil going on around him. Only one who has love at his core and who is love could do anything so great, whilst in such pain.

At the crucifixion, Jesus was powerless and entirely in the hands of others. He was so weak from being flogged and beaten that he could not carry his cross all the way from Pilate's fortress to Calvary. The only active thing Jesus did during this part of his ordeal was to refuse a drink of wine vinegar, which was to numb the pain of his crucifixion. It shows Jesus' determination to drink the cup of suffering that his heavenly Father had placed before him. Even in his weakness and powerlessness, he was obedient to his Father and to carrying out his Father's will – despite the cost to himself. Jesus experienced the pain and suffering in full so that we could experience his redemption in full.

09:00 Hours to 10:00 Hours

The first thing Jesus did on the cross was to look to heaven and address his Father in prayer. He did not pray for himself as he drank the cup he had asked his Father to take away, just a few hours earlier. Jesus did not ask God to take him down from the cross or deliver him from his sufferings. In Gethsemane he had asked for his Father's will to be done and had submitted himself to his Father's will being done. Now it was being done. In the heights of excruciating pain (the pain he had dreaded and agonised over in Gethsemane), he allowed his Father's will to be done to him. What a Saviour!

He did not pray for himself. He prayed for those who had conspired to have him killed, for those who had agreed to his execution and for those carrying it out. He asked his Father to forgive them and even excused them, *"They do not know what they are doing!"* Jesus had taught forgiveness and now he practised it. Forgiveness is not easy in life, but to be dying in excruciating pain and to forgive those who are causing that pain is something else. To be innocent and dying in excruciating pain, not for oneself, but in the place of others for the sins they have committed, it is off the chart in regard to selfless love and selfless sacrifice. What a wonderful Saviour we have in Jesus!

During his time of ministry on Earth, Jesus had taught, *'Love your enemies and pray for those who persecute you!'* (Matthew 5:44). On the cross, he put those words into practise. He loved and prayed for his executioners and he was loving and praying for us – whose sins had nailed him to the cross. In the depths of excruciating pain, he forgave, loved and prayed for those who had caused his suffering. He added to his verbal teaching the power of example. What a Saviour! He prayed for those responsible for his condemnation and crucifixion. In loving forgiveness, Jesus prayed for those who had acted out of hatred, envy and malice. They needed forgiveness for they were as guilty as could be. As religious leaders of God's chosen people, the Jews, they should have known better and behaved better.

09:00 Hours to 10:00 Hours

It was not only the Jewish leaders, or the crowds of Jews who had called for his death or Pilate who had condemned him who were responsible for Jesus' suffering and death. On the cross, Jesus was the sacrifice for all the sins of all mankind. So, everyone who has sinned or will sin, including you and I were responsible for nailing God's sinless Son to the cross. On the cross, sin is exposed in all its horror as God's pure Son bled and died. On the cross all the love and the full nature of God are revealed in all their glory.

Josephus said, 'It was customary for those being crucified, when the nails were being driven into their hands and feet, to curse their crucifiers and to rail down every evil thought upon them.'[17] However, Jesus did not react with protest – he reacted with prayer and asked his Father to forgive his executioners. In the midst of excruciating pain, Jesus' first thoughts and words were directed to his Father. Despite all he was suffering, he retained his confidence in God and continued to love Him and believe in Him. Jesus did not focus on himself but focused on his heavenly Father and the spiritual needs of those crucifying him. Jesus was not self-centred, but other-centred.

Jesus' clothes were divided

After the four soldiers in charge of Jesus' crucifixion had stripped him of his clothes, nailed him to the cross, fixed Pilate's sign to it and secured the cross uprightly in the ground, they divided his clothes among themselves. Jesus had five pieces of clothing. The soldiers took one each, which left the undergarment remaining. This was a seamless garment, woven in one piece from top to bottom. They did not want to tear the undergarment, so they cast lots to see which one of them would get it (John 19:23-24). The casting of lots for Jesus' clothes fulfilled the prophecy in Psalm 22:18 – *'they divided my garments among them and for my clothing they cast lots.'* Then they sat down to keep watch over him as he hung of the cross. The soldiers would have divided up his clothes shortly after 09:00 Hours.

09:00 Hours to 10:00 Hours

The soldiers took his last earthly possessions. Naked he came into the world and naked he left it. Through him all things were made (John 1:3) and the Earth is God's and all that is in it (Psalm 24:1). Jesus is the richest man who ever lived. On the cross he became poor, so poor even his last vestments of clothing were taken from him: *'Though he was rich, for our sakes he became poor, so through his poverty we might become rich'* (2 Corinthians 8:9). He became poor for us on the cross so we might be eternally rich with him. All God's riches are available to all who believe Jesus is God, who died for our sins and rose again. If he was crucified at 09:00 Hours, his clothes would have been divided at that time.

Pilate's sign on the cross

At crucifixions, the charges against the convicted were displayed on their cross. Pilate's sign on Jesus' cross read: *'Jesus of Nazareth, King of the Jews'* (John 19:19). The sign fixed above his head was written in three different languages:

1. **Aramaic** – the language of the Jews
2. **Latin** – the language of the Roman Empire
3. **Greek** – the language of the Gentiles

Jesus was crucified on a road outside Jerusalem. Many would have seen him as they passed in and out of the city. When the religious leaders saw the sign on his cross, they were livid and went to Pilate to ask him to remove it before too many people saw it. They would have left the site of the Crucifixion and walked back along the road to the city. They would have entered Jerusalem through the Ephraim Gate and taken the fastest route to Pilate's fortress. The narrow streets would have been filled with the crowds attending Passover in Jerusalem. The leaders would not have taken the route Jesus took to Calvary. If that fateful journey took about half an hour then the religious leaders' journey would have taken about twenty minutes[18].

09:00 Hours to 10:00 Hours

When Pilate came out to speak to the Jewish religious leaders, they complained to him that Jesus was not the king of the Jews, but just claimed to be. Pilate told them, *"What I have written, I have written"* (John 19:21-22). After this, the leaders would have returned to Calvary. If the journey to Pilate's fortress took twenty minutes[18], it would have taken the same amount of time to return to Calvary. It would not have taken long for the leaders to gain access and speak with the Roman governor – possibly fifteen to twenty minutes. If so, this event would have lasted about an hour and would have happened in the first hour of Jesus' crucifixion (09:00 Hours to 10:00 Hours).

Jesus committed his mother to John's care

After the soldiers divided Jesus' clothes, he looked down from the cross and saw his mother, Mary and John, the disciple whom he loved, standing nearby. He told Mary, John was now her son and he told John, Mary was now his mother. From that time, John took Mary into his home (John 19:25-27). Seeing them would have been one of the first things Jesus saw from the cross. Matthew 27:35-36 says after they crucified him; the soldiers divided his clothes and sat down to keep watch. It would have been after this that Jesus committed Mary into John's care. His second words from the cross (his first were to ask God to forgive his killers) came as the leaders protested to Pilate.

Suffering excruciating pain, Jesus' first thoughts were for others, not for himself. This is the selfless love of our Lord and Saviour. Jesus' first concern was for those being swept along by sin. His second concern was for his mother. There was little he could do to relieve her torment of watching him suffer so cruelly, but he could safeguard her future. He entrusted Mary to the care of John, the disciple he loved. After honouring and showing his love for his heavenly Father by turning to Him first, he honoured and showed his love for his earthly mother by addressing her next. As the eldest son, he knew Mary had no man to provide for and protect the family once he departed.

09:00 Hours to 10:00 Hours

Jesus entrusted Mary to the care of John, the disciple he loved, who was most like Jesus. He knew he could trust John to love and care for Mary as much as he had loved and cared for her. John called himself, *'the disciple whom Jesus loved'* (John 19:26). He had so received and experienced his love; he identified himself by that love. 'Loved by Jesus' was John's status. That was how he saw himself. It was his identity – first and foremost. It was a far higher identity than being Zebedee's son or being a Jew or a Galilean or a fisherman. It is our status too if we will believe. It would have been as much a blessing for him to care for Mary as it was for her to be cared by him.

There was no self-pity in Jesus during his suffering. His thoughts were for others. His love and care for his mother radiates from the cross. When he entrusted Mary to John's care, it perfectly demonstrated a son's love for his mother. How Mary's soul must have been pierced (Luke 2:35) as she watched the bloodied, beaten and bruised figure of her beloved son dying in excruciating pain on the cross before her eyes. It must have broken her to see his nail-pierced hands and feet and the welts and torn flesh caused by the flogging. The blood must have flowed from Jesus' wounds as readily as the pain overflowed from Mary's heart and ran down her face as tears.

The sword in Mary's soul would have pierced deeper when she saw her son in excruciating pain push up on the nails in his feet to catch a breath in order to commit her to John's care. It is the price she paid for accepting her role as the mother of God's Son, *"Let it be done to me according to your word!"* (Luke 1:38). In excruciating pain, Jesus thought of others. First, he turned to his Father to forgive his killers then he turned to his mother to make sure she was cared for after his departure. What a loving son! Jesus was more concerned about his mother's state of abandonment than he was about his own pain. Jesus would have entrusted his mother Mary to John's care in the first hour of his crucifixion – 09:00 Hours to 10:00 Hours.

09:00 Hours to 10:00 Hours

Passers-by insulted Jesus

As Jesus hung on the cross in excruciating pain, those who passed by the Crucifixion as they made their way in and out of Jerusalem through the Ephraim gate hurled insults at him. They shook their heads and said, *"You who are going to destroy the temple and build it in three days, save yourself! Come down from the cross, if you are the Son of God!"* (Matthew 27:39-40 and Mark 15:29-30). People would have passed by on their way in and out of the city from the time that Jesus was nailed to the cross of Calvary at 09:00 Hours.

The next event the Gospels record after Jesus was crucified and insulted and mocked on the cross is darkness came over all Israel from the sixth hour to the ninth hour (Mark 15:33). If 06:00 Hours is the first hour of a Hebrew day then the sixth hour is 12:00 Hours and the ninth hour is 15:00 Hours. If Jesus was crucified at 09:00 Hours then he would have been insulted by passers-by from 09:00 Hours to 12:00 Hours. The insults would have been hurled at him during the first hour of his crucifixion, from 09:00 Hours to 10:00 Hours.

Religious leaders mocked Jesus

It was not only passers-by who mocked Jesus as he hung on the cross of Calvary. Matthew 27:41-43; Mark 15:31-32 and Luke 23:35 all say that the chief priests, the teachers of the law and the elders of Israel sneered and mocked him. They said, *"He saved others, but he cannot save himself! He's the king of Israel! Let him come down now from the cross, and we will believe in him. He trusts in God. Let God rescue him now, if he wants him, for he said, 'I am the Son of God.'"* The religious leaders would have mocked Jesus from the time he was crucified at 09:00 Hours until the time that darkness fell over all Israel at 12:00 Hours. This mocking and sneering by the religious leaders would have happened in the first hour that Jesus hung on the cross of Calvary, that is, from 09:00 Hours to 10:00 Hours.

09:00 Hours to 10:00 Hours

Soldiers mocked Jesus

When the soldiers in charge of Jesus' crucifixion saw the passers-by and the religious leaders insulting Jesus they were inspired to do the same. They would have known little or nothing about Jesus and his teaching, but they would have noticed that the man they had nailed to the cross was drawing a lot of attention. They had fixed Pilate's sign to the cross saying, 'Jesus is the king of the Jews.' Aware of the charge against Jesus, they taunted him with it, *"If you are the king of the Jews save yourself!"* (Luke 23:36-37). They may have offered him a drink when he did not respond to the insults of the passers-by and the religious leaders to moisten his mouth to speak. It did not matter – Jesus did not respond to any of the insults hurled at him from the time he was nailed to the cross at 09:00 Hours, to the time darkness fell over all Israel at 12:00 Hours. The soldiers would have mocked the Son of God in the first hour that he hung on the cross of Calvary, that is from 09:00 Hours to 10:00 Hours.

Two criminals mocked Jesus

In the same way that the passers-by, the leaders, and the soldiers mocked Jesus, the two criminals crucified on either side of him heaped insults on him (Matthew 27:44 and Mark 15:32). Normally victims of crucifixion united by their shared misery cursed and reviled their executioners and onlookers. The two robbers may have been glad that the insults were falling on Jesus and not on them. They had seen the sign on his cross that said Jesus was the king of the Jews. They had heard the insults the passers-by and the Jewish religious leaders had hurled at Jesus as they denounced his kingship and his deity. They decided to join with them. They would have mocked Jesus from the time their ordeal began at 09:00 Hours, until one of the felons acknowledged his deity before darkness fell at 12:00 Hours. The two criminals would have mocked Jesus in the first hour that he hung on the cross, that is, from 09:00 Hours to 10:00 Hours.

10:00-11:00

10:00 Hours to 11:00 Hours

Passers-by insulted Jesus

As Jesus hung on the cross in excruciating pain; passers-by hurled insults at him, saying, *"You who are going to destroy the temple and build it in three days, save yourself! Come down from the cross, if you are the Son of God!"* (Matthew 27:39-40). People would have passed by on their way in and out of Jerusalem from the time that he was crucified at 09:00 Hours until darkness fell over Israel at 12:00 Hours. So they would have hurled insults at Jesus during the second hour of his crucifixion, from 10:00 Hours to 11:00 Hours.

Religious leaders mocked Jesus

Mark 15:31-32 and Luke 23:35 say the leaders sneered and mocked Jesus, saying, *"He saved others, but he can't save himself! He's the king of Israel! Let him come down now from the cross, and we will believe in him."* They admitted he saved others. It is not surprising as the proof was too great to be denied. Yet, when they saw him on the cross, they thought he had lost the power he had. His predicament made him an object of derision. They were so sure he could not come down from the cross, they promised to believe in him if he did. After ridiculing his miraculous powers, they mocked his Messianic claims and blasphemed his divine Sonship with God, *'He trusts in God. Let God rescue him now, if he wants him, for he said, "I am the Son of God!"'* (Matthew 27:43). They believed God had abandoned him and they were God's instruments for punishing him. They were so pleased with themselves, they could wait patiently as they executed God's will then later eat the Passover meal with a clear conscience.

10:00 Hours to 11:00 Hours

Despite all the insults that were thrown at Jesus as he hung on the cross in excruciating pain and despite all the mocking and sneering, he suffered in silence. He did not respond to the foul words of the passers-by or the snipes of the religious leaders. If the Jewish leaders mocked Jesus from the time he was crucified at 09:00 Hours until darkness fell at 12:00 Hours then they would have mocked him in the second hour of his crucifixion, from 10:00 Hours to 11:00 Hours.

Soldiers mocked Jesus

When the soldiers saw passers-by insulting Jesus and the Jewish leaders mocking him, it motivated them to do the same. They had fixed Pilate's sign to the cross which said, 'Jesus is the king of the Jews.' So, they were aware of the charge for which he was being crucified and it was by that title that they taunted him, *"If you are the king of the Jews save yourself!"* (Luke 23:36-37). If the soldiers mocked Jesus from the time he was crucified at 09:00 Hours, to the time darkness fell in Israel at 12:00 Hours, they would have mocked him in the second hour he hung on the cross (10:00 to 11:00 Hours).

Two criminals mocked Jesus

In the same way that the others mocked Jesus, the two criminals being crucified with him heaped insults on him (Mark 15:32). They would have insulted him from the time they were nailed to the cross at 09:00 Hours, until one of them acknowledged that Jesus was the Christ (Luke 23:39-43). If this dying criminal received the revelation that the man hanging next to him was the Son of God before darkness fell over Israel at 12:00 Hours then the two criminals would have insulted Jesus in the second hour that he hung in excruciating pain on the cross of Calvary – from 10:00 Hours to 11:00 Hours.

11:00-12:00

11:00 Hours to 12:00 Hours

Passers-by insulted Jesus

As the Son of God hung on the cross of Calvary in excruciating pain, those who passed by on their way in and out of Jerusalem hurled insults at him. They said, *"You who are going to destroy the temple and build it in three days, save yourself! Come down from the cross, if you are the Son of God!"* (Matthew 27:39-40). If they passed by the Crucifixion from the time he was nailed to the cross at 09:00 Hours until darkness fell at 12:00 Hours, they would have also insulted him during the third hour of his crucifixion – 11:00 Hours to 12:00 Hours.

Religious leaders mocked Jesus

Mark 15:31-32 and Luke 23:35 say that the Jewish religious leaders sneered and mocked Jesus on the cross, saying, *"He saved others, but he can't save himself!* They jeered at his helplessness, yet admitted he had saved others. They had no choice – the evidence was too great to be denied. Seeing Jesus on the cross made them believe he had lost his power and his present situation made him an object of derision. After ridiculing his miraculous powers, they mocked his Messianic claims, *"if he is the king of Israel, let him come down from the cross then we will believe him.'* They called him, 'the King of Israel' not 'the King of the Jews.' They were so sure he could not come down, they promised to believe in him if he did. On the third day, the greater miracle of his resurrection came, but they still would not believe. They would have mocked him in the last hour before darkness fell in Israel – 11:00 Hours to 12:00 Hours.

11:00 Hours to 12:00 Hours

Soldiers mocked Jesus

After the passers-by and the Jewish religious leaders had mocked Jesus as he hung on the cross; Luke 23:36-37 says that the soldiers in charge of his crucifixion also came up and mocked him. They offered him wine vinegar and said, *"If you are the king of the Jews, save yourself."* The soldiers would have known little or nothing about Jesus and his teaching, but they would have seen the man they had nailed to the cross was drawing a lot of attention. They had attached Pilate's sign to the cross which read, 'Jesus is the king of the Jews.' So they would have been aware of the charge for which he was being crucified. It was that name, 'the king of the Jews,' by which they taunted him. If the soldiers mocked him from the time he was crucified at 09:00 Hours until the time darkness fell in Israel at 12:00 Hours then they would have mocked the Son of God in the third hour that he hung on the cross, that is, from 11:00 Hours to 12:00 Hours.

Two criminals mocked Jesus

In the same way that the passers-by, the religious leaders, and the soldiers mocked Jesus, those who were being crucified with him also heaped insults on him (Matthew 27:44 and Mark 15:32). It was the usual practise of those who were being crucified to hurl insults and shout curses at their executioners and at anyone who stopped to stare as they passed by. Normally the victims were united in their shared misery. The two criminals being crucified with Jesus should have been grateful the insults were falling on the man being crucified between them and not on them. Whatever their thinking, they chose to insult him as well. They would have done this from the time they were nailed to their crosses at 09:00 Hours, until it was revealed to one of them, that Jesus was the Christ, the Son of God (Luke 23:39-43). If the revelation came before darkness fell in Israel at 12:00 Hours then the two criminals would have insulted Jesus in the third hour that he hung on the cross, that is from 11:00 Hours to 12:00 Hours.

11:00 Hours to 12:00 Hours

Jesus saved a dying criminal

Matthew 27:44 and Mark 15:32 say both men crucified with Jesus heaped insults on him from the time he was crucified at 09:00 Hours until one of them had a change of heart. It seems he saw, heard and experienced something during this ordeal that revealed Jesus was the Christ, the Son of God. The two felons had seen the sign on Jesus' cross, saying he was the king of the Jews. They had heard his words and the insults that had been hurled at him and turned these things over in their minds. Each one's thoughts produced a different result. Instead of cursing and reviling his executioners and onlookers – one of them reviled Jesus, asking sarcastically, *"Aren't you the Christ?"* Then he mocked him, saying, *"Save yourself!"* As an afterthought the robber added, *"And us!"* (Luke 23:39). However, Jesus ignored him.

The other robber rebuked him, *"Don't you fear God, seeing that you are under the same sentence."* He was saying, "You may not fear God but you will be facing Him very soon. In view of your imminent death and judgment you might at least fear Him and not incur the guilt of reviling this fellow victim." It was fine for the passers-by, the Jewish leaders and the soldiers to mock Jesus. They could do so with a feeling of impunity. It was not the case for the thieves who were dying next to Jesus. He added, *"We are being punished justly, for we are receiving what our deeds deserved, but he has done nothing wrong."* (Luke 23:40-41). He had led a sinful life until justice overtook him. Now he was dying for his sins on a cross. At that moment, instead of mocking Jesus, he opened to the possibility the man dying next to him was who he said he was, and whom the others who had mocked him said he was – the Christ, the Son of God. He confessed his sins and accepted his suffering as a just punishment for his wickedness. As this felon hung dying on a cross, he proclaimed his belief in Jesus' innocence then professed his belief in his divinity by asking, *"Jesus, remember me when you come into your kingdom!"* (Luke 23:42).

11:00 Hours to 12:00 Hours

Pilate's sign on the cross, which read, 'The king of the Jews' would have informed this dying thief of the charge for which Jesus had been condemned to die by crucifixion. He would have heard the passers-by insult Jesus; the religious leaders sneer at him and the soldiers mock him and seen he made no response. He would have heard the leaders call him the king of the Jews and the Son of God. He would have heard Jesus call God, 'Father' and ask him to forgive his killers before he entrusted his mother into his disciple's care.

All that this thief saw and heard helped him to repent – to change his mind. He changed his mind from the belief that the man dying next to him was a criminal being punished for his crimes and deserving of death and worthy of mocking to the belief that the man dying next to him was innocent and who was suffering unjustly was the Christ, the Son of God. Whatever he saw or heard, it made the felon take his mind off his own pain and fix it on Jesus to speak to him. It would have been such a painful ordeal for this thief to speak. He would have had to have pushed down on the nails in his feet to inhale breath, in order to speak. It would have intensified the pain shooting through his body, but he believed it was worth it in order to speak to Jesus.

This thief did not ask much of Jesus and he asked it in such a way that it left the outcome to the Lord. He asked simply that he should give him a thought and not forget about him when he came in his kingdom. With his newfound faith in Christ, he ignored his present situation and suffering to focus on his future. He believed Jesus was the Christ who would return in glory with his Messianic kingdom. As the robber looked at Jesus, he saw a man who on all appearances was condemned as a criminal by his own people and by the Roman authorities suffering and dying on a cross, reviled and mocked by all but a few. However, the dying thief professed his belief that Jesus was the Christ, the Son of God, who was God and he begged him to remember him at the time of his glorious return.

11:00 Hours to 12:00 Hours

Salvation is now

The thief said he was guilty and deserved punishment, but Jesus was suffering even though he was innocent. His faith was rewarded when Jesus said, "*Today, you will be with me in paradise*" (Luke 23:43). It shows we are not saved by being perfect or by obeying religious rituals. Salvation is received through a humble, penitent heart that needs forgiveness and acknowledges Jesus is the Son of God who is God. '*Today*' shows salvation is immediate and present. There is no delay between the thief's request and Jesus' response. He did not say he did not have enough time to be saved or should have asked earlier. Salvation never asks us to become better before coming to God. He does not put us on moral probation or postpone acceptance until a painful or long process of purification has been completed. Salvation is now! For this dying thief, salvation was there to be taken, there and then. If he had waited, he would have missed it, thankfully he did not. God responds to any cry for salvation immediately and he deposits the gift of eternal life into our souls and gives us his Spirit.

The felon may have been losing his physical life but he found eternal life. He showed us how to be saved. He realised who Jesus was and what a sinner he was. He recognised Jesus as Lord and Saviour – the Christ, God's Son. Jesus did not condemn him for his sins, but blessed him with eternal life. His love shown here proves no matter how much we mess up, we are never beyond his redemption. When we see God's Son dying on the cross for our sins, we see God's love for us and His grace to us. When we see the love behind the cross, the love of the God who sent His Son to die for us, it causes us to repent. We see we are sinners who cannot save ourselves and we need a Saviour – Jesus. The revelation to see Jesus dying for our sins comes from God. It is not of us or from us. He made it personal and intimate to us, "*You will be with me...*" Jesus' salvation is a personal relationship. At the heart of salvation is God's Son, Jesus.

11:00 Hours to 12:00 Hours

God's heart was revealed when His Son died on a cross for our sins. At the heart of salvation is a personal relationship with God. *"Eternal life is that they might know you Father and the one you sent, Jesus."* (John 17:3). This relationship begins in this world and lasts forever in the next. Salvation is personal: *'Jesus loves me and gave himself for me.'* (Galatians 2:20). We will not rest content until we call it ours. It is never too late to receive it, as this thief showed. He asked for something in the indefinite future, but received all he asked for and more that day. One thief accepted Jesus' offer of eternal life and the other did not. He refused to submit to Jesus and insulted him instead. He asked Jesus to save him, but his heart was not in the request. He mocked him, *"Save yourself if you are the Christ!"* It was as if he was saying, "yes and whilst you are saving yourself, save us!" He was not making his request in submission to him. It was a selfish plea from an unrepentant heart. As Jesus never answered him, he died unsaved. That criminal showed no fear of God and no remorse for his sin. He knew he was dying, yet he remained defiant.

This scene on the cross was executed by men, but orchestrated by God. Jesus was crucified between two robbers as a lasting picture for us. Both felons began their ordeal in the same position but ended it in very different ones. One went to hell and the other to heaven. One remained defiant to the end and faced eternal separation from God in hell. The other humbled himself, submitting to Jesus' sovereignty and entered eternal life. We have the same choice as the felons. We can refuse to believe and spend eternity in hell separated from God. We must always remember that hell is such an awful, hideous place that even demons do not want to go there (Luke 8:31). Or we can choose to believe Jesus is the Son of God, who is God, who died for our sins on that cross and rose on the third day so we can have everlasting life along with God in heaven. Jesus would have granted eternal life to this dying felon in the final hour before darkness descended over all Israel, that is from 11:00 Hours to 12:00 Hours.

12:00-13:00

12:00 Hours to 13:00 Hours

Darkness came over Israel

From the sixth to the ninth hour darkness came over Israel, as Jesus hung on the cross (Matthew 27:45; Mark 15:33 and Luke 23:44-45). If the sixth Hebrew hour is 12:00 Hours in Western time and the ninth hour is 15:00 Hours, darkness fell from 12:00 Hours to 15:00 Hours. The sudden fall of darkness brought to an abrupt halt the continuous onslaught of mocking and insulting Jesus. A solemn and dreadful silence now loomed over everything for three hours. As the Son of God bled and died on the cross of Calvary, the midday sky in Israel became as black as midnight. When he was born in Bethlehem in a stable, the midnight sky became as light as midday when it filled with angels to announce his birth to the world (Luke 2:9). What a contrast!

The darkness that fell in Israel represented the darkness that fell on Jesus as he took on all the sin and sickness of the world and was separated from his Father as He had to look away from His beloved Son. This was the pain Jesus dreaded most when he agonised in the Garden of Gethsemane. Yes, there was the pain of his betrayal by Judas, his desertion by the apostles and Peter's denials. Then there was the pain and shame of his arrest and trials. There was the physical pain of him being spat on, slapped, punched and beaten. There was the pain of his flogging, having a crown of thorns impaled on his head, of being struck repeatedly on the head with a staff, the pain of carrying his cross, being nailed to it and hanging on it. Yet, none of that pain compared with Jesus, the sinless Son of God being separated from his loving, heavenly Father and the Holy Spirit.

12:00 Hours to 13:00 Hours

In the Bible, darkness is a symbol of sin, judgment and separation from God. Darkness fell that day when the bond between God the Father and His Son Jesus Christ was broken (temporarily). Jesus had the sin of the world laid on him and his holy, heavenly Father could not look on sin. He had to look away from His Son. The Father and the Holy Spirit were obligated to treat Jesus as the worst of sinners. Though Jesus was suffering excruciating physical pain, this paled to the pain he suffered spiritually when he bore our sins on the cross and was separated from his heavenly Father and the Holy Spirit.

What a shock this was to God's sinless Son. He had never sinned, yet all sin was laid on him. He bore the full responsibility and guilt of our sins. He took it all on himself alone. He had never experienced loneliness. Yet his dying on the cross for our sins separated him from his Father and the Holy Spirit – whom he had loved and who had loved him always and with whom he had always had perfect union. This union was broken as our sins were laid on Jesus. How hard this separation must have been and our sin caused it. Jesus became our sin that we might become his righteousness. It is enough to make us turn from sin and turn to God who went through all of this pain for us.

Jesus became sin on the cross. He took on the sin of everyone – all the sins that have been committed, are being committed, and will be committed by all people, past, present and future. Also, it means that Jesus took on the sin of the most evil people who have ever lived. On that cross he became the worst sinner who has ever lived and their sins along with ours were laid on him. The physical pain he suffered was nothing compared to the infinitely greater spiritual suffering of being separated from God his Father. It was a pain Jesus willingly suffered so that we do not have to suffer it. If darkness fell over Israel from 12:00 Hours to 15:00 Hours then the first hour of darkness would have taken place from 12:00 Hours to 13:00 Hours.

13:00-14:00

13:00 Hours to 14:00 Hours

Darkness came over Israel

From the sixth Hebrew hour (12:00 Hours) to the ninth Hebrew hour (15:00 Hours) darkness fell in Israel, as Jesus bled and died on the cross of Calvary (Matthew 27:45; Mark 15:33 and Luke 23:44-45). None of the Gospels record any events taking place during this time of darkness. To pay the price for sin – our sins and the sins of the world – Jesus, the Son of God had to die on the cross of Calvary. God is holy and just. He could not leave our sins unpunished. They had to be paid for. If He did not punish them, He would not be a just God. Yet out of His great love, He decided not to punish us for our sins or punish our sins in us, He punished them in His beloved Son. Jesus' death had to be absolutely horrible because sin is absolutely horrible.

Jesus' death was the penalty that had to be paid to satisfy God's justice against sin and His wrath against sin. The eternal God, the Creator of the universe set the price Himself and He paid the price Himself in the death of His beloved Son, Jesus Christ. During those hours of darkness, Jesus became the Lamb of God who takes away the sins of the world. As God's Son, Jesus had always called God, 'Father.' However, as His sacrifice for sin, Jesus addressed Him as 'God.' Jesus, as God's sacrificial lamb became sin in order to redeem sinful men to a right relationship with the Living God. Because of the sin that was laid on sinless Jesus, God had to look away from him. If darkness fell from 12:00 Hours to 15:00 Hours, he would have hung on the cross in the dark from 13:00 Hours to 14:00 Hours.

13:00 Hours to 14:00 Hours

As Jesus bore our sins in his body on the cross of Calvary, he was separated from his Father and the Holy Spirit for three hours. It seems a short period of time, but if that separation is viewed from an eternal perspective it is another matter. In God's sight, a thousand years are like a day and a day is like a thousand years (Psalm 90:4). If Jesus and his Father were separated for three hours, it is one eighth of a day. In eternal terms, where a day is like a thousand years, one eighth of a thousand years is a hundred and twenty-five years. It gives this pain, separation and aloneness that Jesus suffered a totally different perspective. It was a pain he willingly suffered to restore us to a right and ongoing relationship with his heavenly Father. What a Saviour!

The Gospels record no events during this time of darkness. Jesus is *'the Lamb of God who takes away the sins of the world.'* To take those sins away – to take away our sins, Jesus had to die the most painful of deaths on the cross of Calvary. God is holy and just. He could not leave our sins unpunished. They had to be paid for. If He did not punish them, He would not be a just God. So, out of His great love, He decided not to punish us for our sins or punish our sins in us. He punished them all, past, present and future in His Son Jesus.

Jesus' death was the penalty that had to be paid to satisfy God's justice and His wrath against sin. God set the price Himself and paid the price Himself in the death of His beloved Son. During the hours of darkness (12:00 Hours to 15:00 Hours), during this time of separation between the Son and God his heavenly Father, God poured out his wrath and anger at sin on His sacrifice for sin – Jesus the Lamb of God. God's sacrificial lamb became sin to redeem sinful men to a right relationship with God. Because of the sin laid on sinless Jesus, God his Father had to look away from His Beloved Son. If darkness fell in Israel from midday to 15:00 Hours, Jesus would have borne our sins in his body from 13:00 Hours to 14:00 Hours.

14:00-15:00

14:00 Hours to 15:00 Hours

Darkness came over Israel

Darkness fell over Israel from 12:00 Hours to 15:00 Hours as Jesus hung on the cross (Mark 15:33). The Gospels record no events in this time of darkness. To atone for our sins, Jesus had to die on a cross. God is holy and just. He could not leave our sins unpunished. They had to be paid for. If He did not punish them, He would not be just. Yet out of His great love, He did not punish us for our sins or punish them in us, He punished them in His Son. Jesus' death was the price that had to be paid to satisfy God's justice and His wrath against sin.

God Himself set the price and God Himself paid it, in the death of His beloved Son. During the three hours of darkness (12:00-15:00 Hours), Jesus became the Lamb of God. As His sacrificial lamb, he became sin in order to redeem mankind to a right and ongoing relationship with God. When we repent of our sins and believe Jesus is the Son of God, who is God and we believe and trust in his finished work on the cross of Calvary, we receive all the benefits of his sacrifice – the forgiveness of all our sins, past, present and future; eternal life and healing of all our sicknesses and diseases. Jesus is the same today as he was yesterday and will be tomorrow. He healed all sicknesses and diseases in his time on Earth and he heals them all today. Because of the sin laid on sinless Jesus, his pure and holy heavenly Father had to look away from him. As God could not look on sin, He would have looked away from His beloved Son during the third hour that darkness came over Israel (14:00 Hours to 15:00 Hours).

14:00 Hours to 15:00 Hours

"My God, my God, why have you forsaken me?"

During the three hours of darkness, the intolerable pain of our sins and sicknesses and diseases weighed on Jesus. For three hours he suffered the unbearable pain of separation from his heavenly Father and the Holy Spirit. The judgment of all the sins ever committed by anyone who has, who is or whoever will live on planet Earth was laid on Jesus. For three hours, the absolute fullness of God's wrath and fury against sin were poured out on Jesus as he hung on the cross in excruciating pain. With the pain of the ordeal at its highest, Jesus was totally alone. He was absolutely isolated and in total separation. Jesus was separated from all that was holy, pure and good and was swamped by all that is dark, sinful, evil, hideous, painful and deadly.

After three hours, words exploded from his lips. Abandoned as a Son, He cried out from the pit of his soul and from the brokenness of his heart, *"My God, my God why have you forsaken me?"* (Mark 15:44). Never have more pain-filled words been uttered on Earth – and they were uttered by its Creator. Never had an eternal relationship been broken in such a painful way. Never had one man been so isolated, so abandoned and so alone as the full horror of sin weighed on him as all the force of divine wrath and fury at sin were poured out on him.

He became our sin and our sin separated him from his Father, who had loved him always. Jesus was forsaken by his Father as he took on our sins and died for them on the cross of Calvary. Because Jesus died in our place, we will never die. Because he was forsaken by his heavenly Father, we will never be forsaken by our heavenly Father. Up to this time, Jesus had always called God, 'Father.' During these hours of darkness, he called Him, 'God'. At that moment in time, he was God's sacrificial lamb and addressed Him as the sacrifice for all men's sins and not as His Son. If Jesus died for the sins of the world at 15:00 Hours (Luke 23:44-46), he would have cried this before then.

14:00 Hours to 15:00 Hours

"I thirst"

In order to fulfil all Scripture, Jesus said, "*I thirst.*" Someone near the cross dipped a sponge in wine vinegar and offered it up to his lips. After Jesus had received it, he said, "*It is finished.*" Then he bowed his head and gave up his spirit (John 19:28-30). According to John, Jesus said, "*I thirst*", just before he died. If he died at 15:00 Hours then he would have said this at that time. Mark 15:35-37 say after he asked why God had forsaken him, some onlookers thought he was asking Elijah to rescue him. A man filled a sponge with wine vinegar and offered it to Jesus then with a loud cry he breathed his last. So Mark confirms what John wrote about Jesus being offered a drink before he died. Before saying, '*I thirst*!' as he hung on the cross in excruciating pain, he put his killers, his mother and a dying thief's needs before his own – and even then it was to fulfil Scripture. This selfless, sacrificial love inspires me to follow Jesus and enables me to follow him.

"It is finished!"

The drink Jesus took would have eased the dryness in his mouth and throat to allow him to declare his eternal victory over sin and death. He cried, "It is finished!" Indeed, it was finished. He had taken on himself the sin of the whole world and borne God's wrath and fury against sin and he had paid the price. Jesus God's Son, who is God, paid the price God set against our sin. He paid the price in full to wipe out the debt we owed God for our sin. The work, his Father had sent him to do on Earth was done. His finished work on the cross of Calvary means he paid fully for our total forgiveness, our total righteousness and our total healing. Jesus' death on the cross met all the righteous requirement of the Law. Jesus paid our debt in full. After Jesus said, "*It is finished!*" (John 19:30), he bowed his head onto his chest and gave up his spirit. If he died at 15:00 Hours, then he would have said, "It is finished!" at that time. Mark 15:37 also says that after being offered a drink, Jesus cried out then he died.

14:00 Hours to 15:00 Hours

"Father, into your hands I commit my spirit!"

Luke 23:44-46 says darkness came over the whole land until the ninth hour and the temple curtain was torn in two. Jesus called out with a loud voice, "*Father, into your hands I commit my spirit!*" When he had said this, he breathed his last. John 19:30 says once Jesus had received the drink, he said, "*It is finished!*" With that he bowed his head and gave up his spirit. Matthew 27:50 and Mark 15:37 both confirm that after Jesus had been offered a drink, he cried out and breathed his last. Then they say the temple curtain was torn in two.

The ninth hour in the Hebrew day is 15:00 Hours in Western time. Jesus would have said, "*Father, into your hands I commit my spirit!*" at that time. Jesus' last words before he died were to his Father. His Father had filled his thoughts throughout his life and now they filled his thoughts in his death. Living or dying, Jesus did it all for his Father. In his final moments he could commit himself into the hands of his Father because all of his life he had committed himself into His hands. Jesus began his crucifixion in communion with his Father and he ended it in communion with his Father. That one word, '*Father*' showed Jesus' willing acceptance of the experience he was about to go through and the experience he went through. It shows the heartfelt union of Jesus' will and his Father's will – what a loving, obedient Son!

15:00 Hours

15:00 Hours

Jesus died on the cross

Matthew 27:50 and Mark 15:37 say after Jesus asked God why He had forsaken him, he cried out in a loud voice and breathed his last. Luke 23:46 says after he had committed his spirit into his Father's hands he breathed his last. After he said, *"It is finished!"* he bowed his head and gave up his spirit (John 19:30). The Gospels agree Jesus, the Son of God died on the cross at Calvary for the sins of the world at the ninth hour (15:00 Hours). It was the time the Passover lambs were sacrificed in the temple. That Friday, at 15:00 Hours, Jesus was sacrificed as the ultimate Passover Lamb. In the past the death of a sacrificial lamb had atoned for the sins of one man or for the sins of a family or even for the sins of a nation. The death of Jesus Christ, the Son of God atoned, once and for all, for the sins of the whole world.

The Greek translation of John 19:30 says, Jesus placed his head on his chest then gave up his spirit. This contrasted to how victims of crucifixion usually died. They would throw their heads back in great pain as their struggle to draw in breath ended. Jesus was in charge of his own death and he is in charge of death itself. He chose when to die. He had done all that his heavenly Father had sent him to do including dying for six hours on the cross of Calvary. Now he could return to his Father in heaven. The debt was paid. Jesus paid the debt to God for our sin. He chose to die at the time the Passover lambs were slaughtered at the temple. He was the ultimate Passover Lamb to atone for the sins of the world. Jesus atoned for every sin ever committed by all who have lived, who are living or who will live.

15:00 Hours

The temple curtain was torn in two

As Jesus died at 15:00 Hours, the curtain in the temple was torn in two, from top to bottom (Mark 15:38), revealing it was torn from above. It concealed God's presence and the 'Ark of the Testimony' from view in the inner sanctuary of the temple in Jerusalem. Only the high priest entered 'God's presence' once a year to sprinkle animals' blood on the Ark's cover to atone for his and Israel's sins.

Tearing the curtain in the temple showed Jesus' death had destroyed for all time the dividing barrier (sin) between God and man. Now any repentant sinner could enter God's presence in the Holiest of Holies in the heavenly realms. Sin no longer had to be atoned for once a year by the high priest. Jesus Christ, our great High Priest made atonement for all our sins once and for all. Acts 3:1 says 15:00 Hours was the time of prayer at the temple in Jerusalem. Jesus died at the Passover when the city was full of people attending that feast. Many of them would have been at the temple when the curtain tore. It would have made it difficult for the priests to cover up the event.

Holy people came to life

When Jesus died at 15:00 Hours, the ground shook, rocks split, tombs broke open and many holy men came to life. On the third day, after Jesus Christ, the Son of God had been raised from the dead, these holy men appeared to people in Jerusalem. Only Matthew 27:51-53 says there was an earthquake when Jesus died and Matthew 28:2 says there was an earthquake when he rose to life again. It shows that Jesus' death and resurrection shook the natural world to its core. The natural order had been smashed to pieces as Jesus defeated sin and death on the cross. Then he trampled them under his feet when he rose again victorious on the third day. Death has lost its power. It could not hold Jesus. It could not hold those holy men that day and it cannot hold us. What a victorious Saviour we have in Jesus Christ.

15:00 Hours

The centurion's testimony

When Jesus died at 15:00 hours, the centurion called him the Son of God (Mark 15:39). He would have seen many men die, but not in the way Jesus died. He would have noticed Jesus did not curse during his painful ordeal. He would have heard him call God, 'Father' as he forgave his killers. He would have heard Jesus entrust his mother into his disciple's care before granting salvation to a dying felon. He would have seen him bow his head as he gave up his spirit – not throwing it back to gasp a final breath like other victims. He would have seen darkness fall and felt the ground shake and seen the rocks split and reasoned that Jesus' death was the cause of it all. His words reveal the true power of the Crucifixion. What he witnessed as Jesus died on the cross made him declare that Jesus was God. He was not a Jew, yet because of what he saw at the Crucifixion caused him to acknowledge Jesus' deity. It shows his death on the cross opened salvation's door and restored an ongoing relationship between God and man to both Jews and non-Jews. What a Saviour!

When we fix our eyes on Jesus dying on the cross for our sins, what revelation it brings. A centurion is an unexpected source for such a declaration. They are the words of one of Jesus' killers, a non-Jew. He affirmed him as God's Son. The third man to do so in the Gospels (Peter and Nathaniel were the others – Mark 8:29 and John 1:49). He recognised Jesus as God's Son by the way he died. He died feeling-God-forsaken, yet the soldier saw him as God's Son. Jesus died experiencing God's absence. To the centurion his death revealed God's presence. Jesus felt the absence of God. The soldier felt the presence of God. The cross is a symbol of both the absence and the presence of God. God is present in those conditions that speak most powerfully and tragically of His absence. Through Jesus' suffering, God identifies with human suffering and He becomes one with us. The centurion would have said this at 15:00 Hours

15:00 Hours

The crowd at the cross

When all those who had gathered to witness the Crucifixion saw what had taken place, they beat their chests then went away. But all those who knew Jesus, including the women who had followed him from Galilee, stood at a distance, watching these things. Among them were Mary Magdalene, Mary the mother of James and Salome. In Galilee, these women had followed Jesus and cared for his needs. Many other women who had come up with Jesus to Jerusalem were also there (Luke 23:48-49 and Mark 15:40-41). These women stayed with Jesus to the last. These events would have occurred just after Jesus Christ died for the sins of the world on the cross of Calvary at 15:00 Hours.

The perfect sacrifice by the perfect sacrifice

At the Crucifixion, the full fire and fury of God's wrath fell on Jesus. In the Old Testament, the fire of God's wrath fell on Elijah's sacrifice on Mount Carmel and completely burned it up (1 Kings 18:38). The fire of God's wrath and anger against sin fell on Jesus – God's sacrificial lamb on the cross of Calvary. The sacrifice of Jesus, the Lamb of God – the Son of God and the Son of Man was so perfect that the fire of God did not consume the sacrifice – the sacrifice consumed the fire of God's wrath against sin, evil, sickness, disease and death. The fire of His wrath was totally burned up in Jesus on the cross of Calvary. It was the perfect sacrifice by the perfect sacrifice.

Because Jesus bore away all of God's wrath and anger against our sins, God cannot be angry at our sin anymore. All his anger at our sin was burned up in Jesus when he died for our sins on the cross of Calvary. The price for all of our sins, past, present and future is paid. Jesus was punished for them all. God is holy and just. He cannot punish us twice for our sins. He cannot punish us for sins that have already been punished in His Son on the cross of Calvary. What a perfect Saviour and what a perfect redemption he achieved.

15:00-16:00

15:00 Hours to 16:00 Hours

The bodies on the crosses

The day on which Jesus died was the Day of Preparation. As the next day was to be a special Sabbath, it means he died on Friday. Because the leaders did not want the bodies left on the crosses on the holy day, they went to Pilate and asked to have the legs broken of those being crucified and the bodies taken down from the crosses (John 19:31). For a victim to inhale during crucifixion, he would push up on the nails impaled in his feet. He would be unable to do this if his legs were broken and as a result, he would suffocate and die.

After leaving Calvary, the leaders would have walked along the road to Jerusalem and entered the city through the Ephraim Gate. They would have taken the shortest route through the capital's narrow streets to Pilate's Antonia fortress. If they took the same route as the leaders who had protested to Pilate about his sign saying, 'Jesus is king of the Jews', their journey would have taken about twenty minutes[18]. As leaders of the Jews, they would have gained entrance into Pilate's fortress and an audience with him quite quickly. The Roman governor agreed to their request and sent soldiers to break the victims' legs. Fifteen to twenty minutes is a fair estimate for the time it would have taken to gain access and speak with Pilate. If the leaders took the same route back to Calvary then the journey would have taken about twenty minutes. Overall this event would have lasted about an hour and it would have taken place in the first hour after Jesus Christ died, that is from 15:00 Hours to 16:00 Hours.

15:00 Hours to 16:00 Hours

Jesus' side was pierced

When the soldiers arrived at Calvary, they broke the legs of the men who had been crucified with Jesus. When they came to Jesus, they found he was already dead. They did not break his legs, but one of them pierced his side with a spear. It brought a flow of blood and water (John 19:32-37). These things happened so the Scriptures would be fulfilled: *"Not one of his bones will be broken"* (Psalm 34:20) and *"They will look on the one they have pierced"* (Zechariah 12:10). Blood and water separate in the body, only after death. His side would have been pierced in the hour after he died (15:00 to 16:00 Hours).

Jesus' body was pierced five times

During his crucifixion, Jesus' body was pierced the following ways:

Jesus' body was pierced five times

1. Jesus' right hand was pierced with a nail
2. Jesus' left hand was pierced with a nail
3. Jesus' right foot was pierced with a nail
4. Jesus' left foot was pierced with a nail
5. Jesus' side was pierced with a soldier's spear

In the Bible grace is represented by the number five. John 1:17 says grace came in the person of Jesus Christ. Jesus is grace. His dying on the cross of Calvary for our sins is grace demonstrated in its fullest form. God's grace and mercy punished our sins in his beloved Son Jesus and not in us that we might go free. Jesus paid the price for our sins and we go absolutely free; what grace! In a perfect demonstration of grace Jesus suffered the punishment that we deserved for our sins and we receive all the blessings and favour that Jesus deserved. What wonderful, unconditional, undeserved and amazing grace!

16:00-17:00

16:00 Hours to 17:00 Hours

Joseph asked for Jesus' body

As evening approached, Joseph of Arimathea, a prominent member of the Sanhedrin and a secret believer in Jesus went to ask Pilate for his dead body (Mark 15:42-43). If Joseph witnessed the Crucifixion, he would have taken the same route back to the Antonia Fortress as the leaders who had protested to Pilate about his sign on the cross. Joseph would have walked back along the road and entered the city through the Ephraim Gate then he would have taken the quickest route through the crowded streets to Pilate's Antonia Fortress. Earlier it was shown this walk would have taken about twenty minutes[18].

As a leader of the Jewish people, Joseph would not have waited long for an audience with Pilate. The Roman governor was surprised to hear Jesus was already dead, as crucifixions often took days to kill the victims. He summoned the centurion who was in charge of Jesus' crucifixion and asked him if that was the case. When the centurion told Pilate Jesus was already dead, he agreed to Joseph's request (Mark 15:44-45). So these Scriptures confirm Jesus Christ, the Son of God died on the cross of Calvary. If he had not died, Joseph of Arimathea would not have gone to Pilate to ask for his dead body. If Jesus had not died, the centurion would have told Plate that he was not dead. If he had not died then Pilate would not have released his body to Joseph. It would not have taken long to get Pilate to grant his request. Fifteen to twenty minutes would be a fair estimation for the amount of time it would have taken. After receiving Pilate's consent Joseph would have returned to Calvary to bury Jesus' body.

16:00 Hours to 17:00 Hours

Joseph would have left Pilate's presence and crossed the courtyard of the Antonia Fortress before exiting the Western gate and turning right. He would have travelled through the busy, narrow streets of Jerusalem down to the Tyropean Valley that split the city in two. After crossing the valley, Joseph would have headed in the direction of the Ephraim Gate. His progress would have been slowed as he made his way through the heavily populated streets that connected the temple to the main gates in and out of the city. After navigating the incline to the Ephraim Gate, located where the north-south wall met the east-west wall. He would have exited the city along the road leading to Jaffa to the elevated spot where Jesus had been crucified. It would have taken about twenty minutes to get to Calvary[19]. In total, it would have taken Joseph of Arimathea about one hour to travel to and from the Antonia Fortress to get Pilate's permission to bury Jesus' dead body. If Joseph made this trip after the Jewish religious leaders had asked Pilate to take the bodies down from the crosses then this would have happened from 16:00 Hours to 17:00 Hours.

17:00-18:20

17:00 Hours to 18:20 Hours

Jesus' burial

At Calvary, Joseph took Jesus' body down from the cross with the help of Nicodemus. He was the man who had visited Jesus at night at the first Passover after his baptism (John 3:1-21). They would have begun taking Jesus' body down from the cross by drawing the nails out of his feet from the upright. The crossbeam, with Jesus' hands still nailed to it would have been removed from its socket in the upright and lowered to the ground. Then the nails would have been removed from Jesus' hands from the crossbeam of the cross.

The site of the Crucifixion would have been an unsuitable site to prepare Jesus' dead body for burial. Joseph and Nicodemus would have laid it in a cloth and carried it into the garden that contained the tomb Joseph owned. There, they would have washed Jesus' body and dried it. Next, they would have anointed his body with some of the seventy-five pounds of ointment that Nicodemus had brought. It contained myrrh, which was an aromatic resin and aloes, which was scented wood. Then the body would have been wrapped in strips of linen along with more of the ointment that Nicodemus had brought. After his body was fully wrapped in the strips of linen with ointment secreted between the strips then a separate linen cloth would have been wrapped around his head. Then using the larger cloth on which the body was laid, Jesus' body would have been carried to the tomb cut out of rock and laid inside. Joseph and Nicodemus followed the Jewish burial customs of washing, anointing and wrapping his body.

17:00 Hours to 18:20 Hours

At the place where Jesus was crucified, there was a garden, with a new tomb in it, which had been cut out of rock. It was the Jewish Day of Preparation, which was the day before the Sabbath. As the tomb was nearby; Joseph of Arimathea and Nicodemus laid Jesus' body there (John 19:39-42). The women who had followed Jesus from Galilee saw where the two men laid his body (Luke 23:55). Unlike the disciples who fell asleep when they were asked to keep watch whilst Jesus prayed in the garden on the night before he died, the women from Galilee kept close watch throughout his crucifixion and burial.

Joseph and Nicodemus laid Jesus' dead body in the tomb as the Sabbath was about to begin at sunset that day (Luke 23:53-54). The Jerusalem solar calendar says that the sun sets at 18:20 Hours[a] at the time of Passover in the current year. The time of sunsets has not changed over the years. If it sets at that time today, it would have set at 18:20 Hours on the day Jesus, the Son of God died. If Joseph asked Pilate for his dead body from 16:00 Hours to 17:00 Hours; then he and Nicodemus would have prepared his body for burial and placed him in the tomb after that time and before the sun set, that is, from 17:00 Hours to 18:20 Hours.

JESUS ROSE ON THE THIRD DAY HALLELUJAH!!!

Summary of Jesus' final 24 hours

18:20-21:30 Hours – The Last Supper

18:20 Hours	= Jesus arrived at the Upper Room
18:20-18:50 Hours	= Jesus washed his disciples' feet
18:50 Hours	= The Last Supper began
18:50-19:30 Hours	= Jesus predicted his betrayal
19:30-21:30 Hours	= The disciples argued about greatness
19:30-21:30 Hours	= Jesus predicted Peter's denials
19:30-21:30 Hours	= Jesus introduced the New Covenant
19:30-21:30 Hours	= Jesus and his disciples sang a hymn
19:30-21:30 Hours	= He said, "I am the way, the truth and the life"
19:30-21:30 Hours	= Jesus promised the Holy Spirit
19:30-21:30 Hours	= Jesus said, "I am the true vine"
19:30-21:30 Hours	= Jesus said the world would hate his disciples
19:30-21:30 Hours	= Jesus spoke of the Holy Spirit's work
19:30-21:30 Hours	= Jesus prayed
19:30-21:30 Hours	= The disciples found two swords

21:30-01:45 Hours – Gethsemane

21:30-22:00 Hours	= Journey to Gethsemane
21:30-22:00 Hours	= Jesus predicted Peter's denials
22:00-23:00 Hours	= Jesus' first prayer
23:00-24:00 Hours	= Jesus' second prayer
00:00-01:00 Hours	= Jesus' third prayer
01:00 Hours	= Jesus' betrayal
01:00-01:15 Hours	= Jesus' arrest
01:15-01:45 Hours	= Journey to the high priest

01:45-03:00 Hours – Jesus' trials & Peter's denials

01:45-02:00 Hours	= Jesus' trial by Annas
01:45 Hours	= Peter's first denial
02:00 Hours	= Peter's second denial
02:00-03:00 Hours	= Jesus' trial by Caiaphas
02:00-03:00 Hours	= Jesus said he was the Christ
03:00 Hours	= Peter's third denial

03:00-06:00 Hours – Jesus was kept under guard

03:00-05:50 Hours   = Jesus was kept under guard
05:50-06:00 Hours   = Jesus was condemned

06:00-08:30 Hours – Trials by Pilate and Herod

06:00-06:30 Hours   = Jesus was taken to Pontius Pilate
06:00-08:30 Hours   = Judas Iscariot killed himself
06:30-08:30 Hours   = Jesus' trial by Pilate
06:30-08:30 Hours   = Jesus said he was a king
06:30-08:30 Hours   = Jesus' trial by Herod
06:30-08:30 Hours   = Jesus was condemned to die
06:30-08:30 Hours   = Soldiers took charge of Jesus

08:30-09:00 Hours – Journey to Calvary

08:30-09:00 Hours   = Journey to Calvary
08:30-09:00 Hours   = Simon carried Jesus' cross
08:30-09:00 Hours   = A crowd mourned for Jesus

09:00-12:00 Hours – the Crucifixion

09:00 Hours   = Jesus was crucified
09:00 Hours   = Jesus forgave his killers
09:00 Hours   = Jesus' clothes were divided
09:00-10:00 Hours   = Pilate's sign on the cross
09:00-12:00 Hours   = Jesus committed his mother to John's care
09:00-12:00 Hours   = Passers-by insulted Jesus
09:00-12:00 Hours   = The religious leaders mocked Jesus
09:00-12:00 Hours   = The soldiers mocked Jesus
09:00-12:00 Hours   = Two criminals mocked Jesus
09:00-12:00 Hours   = Jesus saved a dying criminal

12:00-15:00 Hours – Darkness came over Israel

12:00-15:00 Hours   = Darkness came over Israel
15:00 Hours   = Jesus' cry of dereliction
15:00 Hours   = Jesus said, "I thirst!"
15:00 Hours   = Jesus said, "It is finished!"
15:00 Hours   = Jesus committed his spirit to his Father

15:00 Hours – Jesus died on the cross

15:00 Hours	= Jesus died on the cross
15:00 Hours	= The temple curtain was torn in two
15:00 Hours	= Holy people came to life
15:00 Hours	= The centurion's testimony
15:00 Hours	= The crowd at the cross

15:00-18:20 Hours – Jesus' burial

15:00-18:20 Hours	= The bodies on the crosses
15:00-18:20 Hours	= Jesus' side was pierced
15:00-18:20 Hours	= Joseph asked for Jesus' body
15:00-18:20 Hours	= Jesus' burial

Timing of final hour events

Events in Jesus' final hours began at 18:20 Hours when he arrived at the house for the Last Supper. They ended at 18:20 Hours the next day when Joseph laid his dead body in the tomb. From 09:00 Hours to 15:00 Hours, Jesus, the Son of God, who is God hung and died in excruciating pain on Calvary's cross for six hours for the sins of the world before he gave up his spirit.

Three-hour timeframes

Many events in the final hours break down into three-hour segments:

Three-hour timeframes

- 3 Hours = The Last Supper
- 3 Hours = Jesus prayed in the Garden of Gethsemane
- 3 Hours = Jesus was kept under guard
- 3 Hours = Trials by Pilate and Herod and journey to Calvary
- 3 Hours = Jesus hung on the cross before darkness fell
- 3 Hours = Darkness fell over all Israel
- 3 Hours = From Jesus' death to his burial

Now the events of Jesus' final hours have been established in an hour-by-hour timeframe, let's see what the final twenty-four hours of Jesus' life reveal about his nature and character and the nature and character of God and of the main people involved in his final hours.

The love and character of Jesus

Final hour events began at the Last Supper and reveal the perfection of Jesus' character and his love for God, his disciples and all people.

Jesus washed his disciples' feet

Jesus knew he would be betrayed by Judas, denied by Peter and deserted by his disciples, but it never stopped him loving them. Before the Last Supper began, he showed them the full extent of his love by washing their feet and drying them with a towel. Jesus, the one true God, the Creator of the universe, the King of kings and Lord of lords took on the role of the lowest servant in a home – the one who washed everyone's feet. Jesus is the Servant King. His life on Earth was one of selfless service, humility and love. He even washed Judas' feet even though he would betray him. Seeing their Lord behave like a slave confused them, especially Peter. They had not understood his teaching that to be a leader they must serve. He wanted them to continue his ministry of service after his departure. They were to serve God, serve each other and serve all people.

The Last Supper

He said how eagerly he had desired to eat the meal with his disciples. It was Jesus' final meal before he died and there was no one he would rather eat it with than them. The Creator of the world – God in human form was delighted to share his last meal with them (and Judas). What a testimony to his love. He could have ate his last meal with rulers but chose to eat it with them.

There is no greater pain (apart from death) than being betrayed by the one you love. If we who love imperfectly are devastated when we are betrayed, how much more pain did he who loves perfectly suffer when his close friend betrayed him. However, he did not highlight Judas' treachery in front of the others. He allowed him to leave unchallenged. Jesus showed such love by honouring Judas even when his actions caused him such anguish. He loved him more than anyone and would have been hurt more than anyone by his betrayal, but it did not stop him loving Judas. Who could love the one who betrayed him to death? Only the love of God in Christ Jesus and he loved Judas to the end.

Jesus predicted Peter's denials

Out of his love for his disciples, Jesus warned Peter, Satan wanted to sift them as wheat. He would test them and they would fail. Jesus knew they would fail, but it would not stop him loving them. He loved them so much he had prayed that their faith would not fail even though Satan wanted to prove it was nothing more than chaff. Then Jesus told Simon that after he had failed and turned back, he was to strengthen his brothers. Even in this warning, he was reassuring Simon that despite his failing, he would still lead his Church, but his words were not received with gratitude. Peter was indignant and refuted his comments, vowing he would go to prison and death with Jesus, but he told him he would deny him three times before the rooster crowed (Luke 22:31-34).

There is pain when a loved one does not listen to advice that will save them suffering. After being with him so long, Peter should have known what Jesus said, happened, be it a miracle catch of fish (Luke 5:1-11), or meeting a man with a water jar (Mark 14:13-16). His pride stopped him heeding Jesus' warning, but it never stopped Jesus' unconditional love flowing to him. Peter was not the only disciple to refute Jesus' words. On the way to Gethsemane, when he said all the disciples would desert him, they swore they would not and would die with him. He knew them better than they knew themselves. He knew how weak they were, yet it did not diminish his love for them. Out of that love, Jesus tried to help them avoid suffering due to their weaknesses and frailties, but they did not listen to him.

Jesus introduced the New Covenant

When instituting the New Covenant, he told his disciples to remember his death on the cross above all else – above his teachings, signs, miracles, and wonders. God himself – came to Earth to die for our sins. His death, his shed blood, frees us from our sins. His death gives us eternal life. His broken body heals all our sicknesses and diseases. His death redeems us from the Curse and restores to us all that was lost in Adam's Fall. It restores our relationship with God. His death achieves all this and so much more. This is why he wanted his disciples (and us) to remember his death above all else. What a wonderful Saviour! What a loving, forgiving God we have!

When Jesus instituted the New Covenant, he broke bread and gave a piece to each of his disciples. He was showing them and us that we are all part of one body – his body. His death on the cross makes us one with him and God. When God made the first covenant with Israel at Mount Sinai, it was sealed with animal's blood. The New Covenant between God and man was sealed with His Son's blood shed for our sins on the cross. The wine in the Communion Cup continually reminds us of God's eternal covenant with us – the forgiveness of our sins through the blood, shed in love by Jesus.

Jesus promised the Holy Spirit

Jesus told his disciples to love each other with the same sacrificial love he had for them and for all people. This love is an attitude that reveals itself in actions. Out of this love, he was going to prepare a place for them in eternity and would return to take them to where he was. He is the way to God, because he is both God and man. By uniting their lives with his they would be united with God always. They would be one, just as he and God were one, to the degree that anyone who had seen him had seen God. He so loved them, he would not leave them as orphans. He would send the Spirit, the third person of the Trinity to be with them forever. To have the Spirit in them was to have Jesus in them – always. If they trusted in his and God's love, they would receive whatever they asked in his name. He told them to love each other as he had loved them. God's Son loved them enough to call them friends and to die for them. This mixed group of Galileans were now friends with God. Then out of his love, Jesus prayed for his friends and for all believers.

Jesus told his disciples to watch and pray

Jesus had warned his disciples about the tests they faced at the Last Supper. In Gethsemane, Jesus told his disciples to watch and pray, so they would not fall into temptation. He said it for their benefit not his, but they neither watched nor prayed and fell asleep. Their prayers were not needed to change the ordeal Jesus faced, but to give them the strength they needed to get through the ordeal they faced. Once again Jesus showed his selfless love for his disciples. He did not want them to be engulfed by what they were about to experience and gave them the tools to help them. They did not listen to him or obey him as they relied on their own strength and as a result they fell fast asleep.

Jesus said his soul was filled with sorrow to the point of death as the anguish of his imminent violent ordeal weighed on him. After expressing feelings of distress and revulsion to his disciples, he expressed them to his Father in prayer, as he submitted to His will. He called on divine power to help him do what was humanly impossible. Only God can enable humans to follow a path of selfless sacrifice, selfless love and suffering. Jesus, who is fully God and fully man asked for the cup to be taken away. As a man, he had natural inclinations and a human will. He submitted himself to God's will and it took a great emotional and mental struggle to achieve it.

When he found his disciples asleep, he lovingly told them to pray for God's strength so they would not fail (Luke 22:40). He had shown this truth as he agonised in prayer. If he needed to pray for God's strength to face his trials, so did they, and to put their confidence and trust in Him, not in themselves. He understood why they had failed to keep watch over him as he had told them. He spent that hour alone, prostrate in prayer. They spent it prostrate in sleep, but still he encouraged them to watch and pray as it is the only way through trials. Good will and intentions can come to nothing in trials due to human weakness. It is what happened to them. He told them to pray so they might have God's power to get through the ordeal. He did not tell them to do anything he did not do himself. It was the prayer that he prayed to God that night.

Jesus faced his vulnerabilities and confronted his convulsion at the prospect of dying as he acknowledged his own fears and fragility. His disciples denied theirs and could not support him in his hour of need. They slept as he prayed. He had asked them to watch and they had failed. In selfless love and humble obedience, he submitted his will. His entire human nature cried out against the idea of suffering and dying. This part of his human spirit and will had to submit fully to God's will, if he was to see his ordeal through to the end. He prayed from the anguish gripping his soul in the struggle to submit his natural inclinations to God's will and accept all the pain of his Passion. The suffering concentrated in his soul overflowed into his body as he sweated blood (Luke 22:39-44). As a result of his prayers, peace reigned in his heart and he fully submitted to his death on a cross. He allowed this suffering of his soul to show how human he is to help us.

Jesus' betrayal and arrest

How painful it must have been for Jesus to have his friend betray him with a kiss, the sign of friendship. He stepped forward to identify himself to the arresting party and told them to let his disciples go. In the face of arrest, trial and death, his thoughts were for others. Out of selfless love, he was more concerned about saving his disciples than saving himself. Jesus submitted to being betrayed and arrested in this manner out of obedience to God and to fulfil all Scriptures. Peter did not see it that way and lashed out with his sword, cutting off a man's ear. Jesus did not need his help. He rebuked Peter then in love healed the ear of his enemy who had come to arrest him.

At the first sign of trouble, the disciples' frailties caused them to desert Jesus, but it did not stop him loving them. It was all part of God's will. He had to go to the cross alone. He alone was worthy to suffer and die for us, but their desertion must have added to his pain. These events reveal Jesus and his disciples' reactions in times of crisis and the latter fell well short. He faced his human frailties and laid them before God. It was a painful, lonely struggle for him in the garden to fully submit to God's will. The result was, in the heat of crisis, when he called on God's power he had the strength to do God's will. His disciples denied their frailties and trusted in their own power to face the crisis and they were exposed as weak and frail.

Jesus' trials by Annas and Caiaphas

God's Son was bound like a criminal and led from Gethsemane to the high priest, Annas. Jesus called him to task when he tried to get him to incriminate himself by telling him about his teachings and his disciples. He told Annas to call witnesses if he had done anything wrong. He rebuked Israel's leading religious figure without fear or hesitation, but an official struck him in the face. It was a cowardly act to strike a bound man. Jesus reacted to this violence in modesty and meekness. His calm logic was a rebuke to the one who struck him and to Annas who had allowed it and let it go unpunished. Jesus had no fear of Annas. He knew he had to die no matter what the result of this trial. After praying and submitting to God's will, he had the strength and peace to endure this. Annas realised he was making him look bad and sent him to be tried by Caiaphas.

He refused to incriminate himself by responding to the false testimonies made against him, so Caiaphas asked Jesus to swear by God if he was the Christ. When he said he was, he was accused of blasphemy and condemned (Mark 14:61-64). The leaders spat in his face, blindfolded him and struck him repeatedly, but he did not lash out or retaliate. He accepted it all in silence. He did this in loving obedience to God and out of love for us. Then guards mocked him, beat him and imprisoned him (Luke 22:63-65). He could have used his position as God's Son to escape, but he chose to stay and suffer the beatings and insults. He did not resist, defend himself or retaliate. His true status and dignity are revealed in the most degrading of circumstances. Out of maturity and human perfection Jesus had no pride, hatred, self-pity or thought for himself. He felt more pity for Peter than himself. After failing him so badly and denying him a third time, Jesus looked at him with such love, it broke him.

Jesus' trials by Pilate and Herod

When the leaders met at dawn to condemn Jesus, they asked him if he was the Christ. He knew they were not seeking the truth about him and said if he told them they would not believe (Luke 22:66-68). They just wanted him dead and took him to Pilate to get him to do their bidding. Jesus behaved with such poise and dignity throughout his trials by Pilate and Herod. Despite the religious leaders vehemently accusing him of all sorts of trumped up charges, he refused to respond. In his trial by Pilate, Jesus showed kindness to the Roman governor when he told him the religious leaders were more guilty than he for condemning him. Pilate responded to his kindness by trying to get him freed. However, he was a weak champion. He gave into the crowd and condemned him to death.

The Crucifixion

At Calvary, Jesus was offered wine and gall to help deaden the pain of his crucifixion. He refused to drink it. He was going to suffer the pain of crucifixion in full consciousness and with a clear mind. Out of his great love for his Father and for sinners like us, he submitted to dying in excruciating pain on the cross. Evil men put Jesus in the middle of two felons to discredit and shame him. God allowed it to happen to show the world Jesus is the centre of all things. Jesus in his love for us wants to be at the centre of our lives too.

Out of his love for God and for us, Jesus submitted to crucifixion. God's innocent Son chose to die in our place that we, the sinners might go free. It is the wonder of the cross and of Jesus' loving, selfless sacrifice. He paid the price and we go free. It is too unbelievable to make up and too sublime for our minds to comprehend. It is God's revelation in the human heart that enables us to see God himself died on a cross for our sins. What amazing grace!

God was willing to let Jesus go as low as possible to redeem sinful men from life's lowest depths and cleanse them of their sins, heal them of their sicknesses and give them eternal life and an unending relationship with Him. The death Jesus died means we can never sink so low as to be beyond God's love or the fullness of His redemption. No one is beyond His love. Jesus died for each of us, to take away our sin and shame. He bore them away in his body on the cross. He died for us. We must go to him in repentance and let him rid us of our guilt and shame and receive life. The new life he gives lasts forever. Each person has such value in God's sight He let His Son die for us. Jesus, in his love for us died with sinners and for sinners.

Jesus hung on the cross

The first person Jesus turned to on the cross was his Father. During his ministry, he had turned to God first. He turned to Him first in death, not for himself, but for his killers – not to condemn them, but to forgive them. He still loved and trusted his Father, despite the evil going on around him. Only one who has love at his core and who is love could do anything so selfless whilst in such pain. Helpless and weak, Jesus was obedient to God and to carrying out His will, despite the cost to himself. He experienced the pain in full, so we could experience his redemption in full. To be innocent and dying in excruciating pain, not for oneself, but in the place of others, for the sins they committed is the perfect display of selfless love and sacrifice. Deep in pain, he forgave those who had sinned, loved his enemies, and prayed for his persecutors. He added to his teaching the power of example. On the cross all the love and nature of God are revealed in their glory. Despite his suffering, Jesus retained his confidence in God and continued to love Him and trust in Him. He did not focus on himself, but on God, and the spiritual needs of his killers.

Jesus committed his mother to John's care

Jesus showed selfless love on the cross when he committed Mary into John's care (John 19:25-27). Suffering excruciating pain, in selfless love, he thought of others, not himself. He could not relieve her torment of seeing him suffer so cruelly, but he could secure her future by placing her into the care of the disciple he loved. On the cross, he loved and honoured his heavenly Father and earthly mother. He knew Mary had no one to provide for her once he was gone. He entrusted her to the care of the disciple most like himself, who would love and care for Mary as much as he had loved and cared for her.

Jesus granted salvation to a dying felon

As Jesus hung on the cross, he suffered in silence as he was mocked by passers-by; the Jewish leaders; the soldiers; and the two criminals. When one of the felons asked him to remember him when he came in his kingdom, Jesus said he would be with him that day in paradise. It shows his acceptance, love and salvation are available to all, no matter how far they have fallen or how bad they have been. He did not have to meet any criteria. He repented of his sin and believed Jesus was the Christ to be saved. God's heart was revealed when His Son died on a cross for our sins. At the heart of salvation is a personal relationship with God. Jesus said, *"Eternal life is that they might know you Father and Jesus, whom you sent"* (John 17:3). This relationship starts in this world and goes on forever in the next. We have the same choice as the felons. We can refuse to believe and spend eternity in hell apart from God. Or we can believe Jesus is God and spend everlasting life with him.

Darkness came over Israel

Darkness fell as Jesus took on all the sin and sickness of the world and was separated from God as He looked away from His beloved Son. It was the pain Jesus had agonised over in Gethsemane – a pain greater than his betrayal, desertion, flogging and crucifixion. Being separated from his Father and the Holy Spirit was the worst pain of all. Because of the sin laid on Jesus they had to look away and treat him as the worst of sinners. All sin was laid on him. As he bore the full responsibility and guilt of our sins alone, it separated him from God.

His dying on a cross for our sins separated him from God and the Spirit whom he had loved and who had loved him always and with whom he had always had perfect union. But this was broken as our sins were laid on him. How hard this separation must have been and our sins caused it. He became our sin, so we might become his righteousness. It is enough to make us turn from sin and turn to God, who suffered all of this pain and death for us. To pay the price for our sins, Jesus had to die on a cross. God is holy and just. Our sins had to be punished. They had to be paid for. If He did not punish them, He would not be a just God. Yet out of His love, He did not punish us for our sins or punish our sins in us, He punished them in His Son. His death had to be absolutely horrible, because sin is absolutely horrible. His death was the penalty that had to be paid to satisfy God's justice and His wrath against sin. God set the price and He paid it in the death of His Son. It was a pain Jesus willingly suffered to restore us to a right relationship with God. What a Saviour!

Jesus' cry of dereliction

The final consequence of sin is separation from God. Jesus suffered that separation for us so that we do not have to experience it. He who had been with his Father always was separated from Him by our sin and for our sin, to pay the price for our sin. He willingly did it out of his love for us. His Father was equally willing to suffer, so He could be in relationship with us forever. We must never forget what it cost God to pay the debt for our sins that we may have eternal life, forgiveness of sins and healing for all our diseases. It cost Jesus his life on a cross.

The fullness of God's wrath against sin was poured out on Jesus for three hours at Calvary. With pain at its greatest, he was separated from all that is holy, pure and good and was swamped by all that is dark, evil and deadly. No wonder he cried from the pit of his soul, "*My God, my God why have you forsaken me?*" (Mark 15:34). Never have more pain-filled words been uttered on Earth and they were uttered by its Creator. Never had one man been so abandoned and so alone as the full horror of sin weighed on him and the full force of God's wrath at sin fell on him. Never had an eternal relationship been broken in such a painful way, yet Jesus submitted to it all out of humble, loving obedience to God and out of his love for us.

Jesus' death

Because he was forsaken by God we will never be forsaken by Him. As Jesus died, he cried, "It is finished!" And it was finished. He had taken on himself the sin of the world and borne God's wrath and fury against it. He paid the price. God's Son, who is God, paid the price God set against our sin. He paid the price in full to wipe out the debt we owed God for our sin. The work God had sent him to do on Earth was done. Jesus' finished work on the cross of Calvary paid fully for our forgiveness, healing and righteousness. His death met all the righteous requirement of the Law. Jesus paid our debt in full.

As Jesus died, he committed his spirit into God's hands (Luke 23:46). His last words were to his Father, who had filled his thoughts throughout his life. Now He filled them in his death. Living or dying, Jesus did it all for his Father. In his last moments he could commit himself into His hands because all his life he had committed himself into His hands. He began his crucifixion in communion with his Father and he ended it in communion with Him. It shows the heartfelt union of Jesus' will and His will – what a loving, obedient Son! In the crowning moment of world history, Jesus, who is God, died for the sins of the world. God's sinless Son became our sin and died for our sin so that we may have eternal life. What love! What selflessness! What grace! He paid and we go free! What an amazing sacrifice!

When Jesus died, the curtain in the temple was torn in two. It showed his death destroyed for all time the dividing barrier (sin) between God and man. Now any repentant sinner could enter God's presence. Sin no longer had to be atoned for once a year by the high priest. Jesus, our great High Priest made atonement for all our sins once and for all. As he died, the ground shook, rocks split, tombs broke open and holy men came to life. On the third day, after Jesus' resurrection, these holy men appeared in Jerusalem (Matthew 27:51-53). It shows Jesus death shook the natural world to its core. The natural order was smashed to pieces when he defeated sin and death on the cross. Death lost its power. It could not hold Jesus. It could not hold those holy men and it cannot hold us. What a Saviour!

The centurion's testimony

When the centurion at the Crucifixion saw how Jesus died, he said he was God (Mark 15:39). It shows his death opened the door to salvation and an ongoing relationship between God and man, to Jews and non-Jews. What a Saviour! Jesus died feeling forsaken by God, yet this soldier saw him as God's Son. He died experiencing God's absence. To the centurion his death revealed His presence. One felt the absence of God and the other felt the presence of God. The cross is a symbol of the absence and the presence of God. He is present in those conditions that speak most powerfully and tragically of His absence. Through Jesus' suffering, the eternal God identifies with human suffering and He becomes one with us.

Jesus chose to die

As the pure Son of God and the sinless Son of Man, Jesus is the only man in all creation who had the choice to accept or reject death. If he had chosen to, he could have bypassed the cross and returned to heaven. We do not have that choice. No one but Jesus had it, for all have sinned and fallen short of the glory of God (Romans 3:23). Death is the result of sin (Romans 6:23) and as we have all sinned, we all die. Jesus never sinned, so death was not inevitable for him. He chose to die out of obedience to God and out of his love for us. He obeyed God's will even though it led to death. Yet death was not the end. He trusted his Father to lead him into death, through death and out of death. It was worth it. His death brought an end to death. He obeyed God, though it cost him everything. The almighty, eternal God was willing to send His One and Only Son, His beloved Son, the One whom He had loved always to die for our sins. What a God!

The fire of God's wrath against sin fell on Jesus, His sacrificial lamb on the cross of Calvary. The sacrifice of Jesus, the Lamb of God – the Son of God and the Son of Man was so perfect that the fire of God did not consume the sacrifice as it did when the prophet Elijah sacrificed a bull to God on Mount Carmel (1 Kings 18:36-38). When God sacrificed Jesus for our sins on the cross, the sacrifice – God's Son consumed the fire of God's wrath against sin, evil, sickness, disease and death. The fire was completely burned up in Jesus, on the cross. It was the perfect sacrifice by the perfect sacrifice.

Key characters in Jesus' final hours

Simon Peter

Let's see what our chronology reveals about the main characters in Jesus' final hours, starting with Peter, whose final hours were not his finest hours. At the Last Supper, he refused to let Jesus wash his feet. He could not bear the idea of he, whom he had said was God, taking a servant's role to wash his feet. Undeterred, he showed Peter he had to learn to submit to him in all things if their relationship was not to be broken – even washing his feet (John 13:1-17). Jesus could take the role of the lowest servant and wash feet because he knew who he was. Washing feet did not change his identity, which was not based on what he did, but on who he was – the Son of God and the Son of Man. Peter's refusal to let him wash his feet shows he did not know who he was or who Jesus was. If he did not have a true assessment of who he was then he did not have a true assessment of others. He thought he knew himself, but events that night show he did not. And he had no real knowledge of Jesus or the purpose of his mission. The King of kings came as a servant king. The eternal God came to serve man. He showed it by washing their feet, but Peter refused to let him. If he would not let him be a servant to him how would he let himself be a servant to anyone? He was telling Jesus what to do and not submitting to him.

Jesus predicted Peter's denials

At the Last Supper, Jesus told Peter Satan wanted to sift him as wheat (Luke 22:31-34). He was warning him, the Devil wanted to crush him to show his faith was not wheat, but chaff, which would be blown away in the wind of testing. He reassured Peter he had prayed for him that his faith would not fail and when he had turned back, he was to strengthen his brothers. He was saying Peter would go through a time of testing and would fail. The good news was he had prayed that his faith would not fail and he would be restored after his fall. Then he was to restore the others. Jesus called him, 'Simon', not the name he had given him: 'Peter'. Peter was the name on which he would build his Church. He called him by his earthly name, Simon, as he would fail through his earthly nature.

Despite this warning, Peter did not thank Jesus for prompting him to be on his guard. He thought he knew better than God. He refuted his words and boasted he was ready to go to prison and even death with him. He was so confident of his love and loyalty to him, there was no possibility in his mind that he would not stand by him in all circumstances, even if it was prison or death. How wrong he was! Events that night showed he was different to the man he believed he was. Jesus knew exactly who Peter was. He knew all his strengths and all his weaknesses and loved him regardless. His love for Peter was so great this was not the only time he warned him that night.

On the way to Gethsemane, Jesus said all his disciples would abandon him (Mark 14:27-31). He made no exceptions. Peter said, *"Even if all fall away on account of you, I will not."* He was willing to put down the others to swear his loyalty to Jesus. His love and zeal were admirable, but his pride was not. Jesus' words offended him and he was belligerent to him. He insisted he was more dependable than anyone else. Then Jesus said, *"I tell you the truth, this very night, before the rooster crows, you will disown me three times."* Peter insisted, *"Even if I have to die with you, I will never disown you."* He did not contradict him. He did not have to. When Jesus spoke, his words took place, be it calming a storm (Mark 4:39) or raising the dead (John 11:43-44). Peter had witnessed that what Jesus said happened, but that night, his pride stopped him believing.

Because of Peter's pride, God allowed him to fall – not too far, but far enough for him to learn humility. No one can doubt his sincerity. The problem was, he was sincerely wrong. He could not comprehend in his heart that he would ever deny Jesus. Peter was sincerely wrong about his assessment of himself and his strength. He was slow to look at his weaknesses, but quick to look at the weaknesses in the disciples and highlight them to make himself look good. He mistakenly compared himself to others when the perfect man stood before him – one who did not think too highly or too lowly of himself. If Peter had compared himself to Jesus then he would have had a true assessment of himself. Peter's problem was that he did not really know himself. He thought he did, however, he did not and soon this seasoned fisherman would learn that painful truth.

Jesus knew himself fully and gave himself fully to God that night. He was fully God and fully man and gave the fully man side of himself fully to God. Peter did not have such a balanced view of himself. He thought too highly of himself. He was overconfident in himself and it caused him to fall. He believed he had the power in and of himself to stand by Jesus, come what may. He did not understand the weakness of his flesh. In his pride and self-righteousness, he believed he was above serious sin – even to the extent of minimising Jesus' words. He was depending on himself, but needed to depend on God for all things. At the Last Supper, Jesus told Peter this when he said he was the True Vine and he could do nothing without him (John 15:5). It seems his words fell on deaf ears.

As Jesus prayed, Peter slept

Peter's ability to listen did not improve in the Garden of Gethsemane. Jesus took him, James and John with him as he prayed. He began to be deeply distressed and troubled and said his soul was overwhelmed with sorrow to the point of death. Then he asked them to keep watch whilst he prayed. After he finished praying, he found the trio sleeping. Jesus asked Peter, *"Could you not keep watch with me for one hour?"*

Peter had failed to do what Jesus had asked him. Yet, in his love for him, Jesus told him to watch and pray so that he would not fall into temptation. Out of his great love for Peter, he was advising his lead disciple that when temptation came he needed to put his confidence and trust in God, not in himself. Instead of displaying his self-declared dependability, he needed to learn the humility and poorness of spirit needed for God to work through him. Then he encouraged Peter with these understanding words, *"The spirit is willing, but the flesh is weak!"* (Matthew 26:36-41 and Mark 14:32-38).

Jesus knew that in his spirit Peter desired to do what was right, but he displayed the weakness that is common to all humanity. Jesus told him to rely on God's strength, but Peter's pride stopped him doing that and he relied on his own strength. He knew Peter needed God's strength not his own to get through the trials he faced and showed this truth as he agonised in prayer. If God's Son needed to pray to God for strength to face his ordeal, so did Peter.

When Jesus found Peter asleep again after his second prayer, he did not know what to say (Mark 14:39-40). He, who always had something to say was silent. On the Mount of Transfiguration, he saw Jesus as almost divine as he shone with glory. He hardly appeared human and Peter was awestruck (Mark 9:5-6). On the Mount of Olives, as Jesus agonised over the forthcoming pain, suffering and death, Peter saw him as fully human and barely divine as he confessed he needed God's strength to get through the pain, suffering and death. Peter did not obey his words and fell asleep.

Man in his nature lacks the discipline and strength to live up to his highest desires. God understands our dilemma. He knows what we are like in our human selves, that we are weak and frail, but He is gracious to us in all ways. Jesus understood why Peter had failed him in not staying awake to watch over him. He spent that hour alone, prostrate in prayer. Peter spent it prostrate in sleep, yet Jesus still encouraged him, saying he needed to watch and pray so he would not fall into temptation. The only way through trials is to watch and pray. Good will and intentions can come to nothing in trials through human weakness. It did for Peter. Jesus told him to pray so he might have God's power to get through the ordeal. He did not pray and he did not have God's power to get through it. He did not tell him to do anything he did not do himself. It was the prayer he had prayed.

Out of his love for Peter, Jesus encouraged him to watch and pray to face the ordeals that lay ahead. God in human form knew the spirit was willing, but the flesh was weak. Peter refused to listen to his warnings. Now he was refusing to listen to his advice. Jesus knew Peter's heart better than himself. Peter should have known that. From the time they met, Jesus had shown he knew more than him when he provided a boat-sinking catch of fish (Luke 5:1-11) on the lake where Peter fished every day in a part of it and at a time when catching fish was impossible. Yet, Peter did not apply that experience to events that night. He should have humbled himself as he did that day, rather than try to prove Jesus wrong. But his own will and determination counted for nothing when he did not take Jesus' advice and fell asleep. How embarrassed he must have been and how shallow his words must have seemed when Jesus woke him after his third prayer.

Peter cut off the high priest's servant's ear

When the leaders, temple guards, elders and soldiers tried to arrest Jesus, his disciples asked him if they should use their swords to defend him. Before he could answer, Peter lashed out and cut off the high priest's servant's ear (Luke 22:49-50) as he showed Jesus he was with him in his hour of need. He was standing by him in the heat of battle, but instead of commendation, he received condemnation for trying to defend him. Jesus told him to put his sword back in its place for all who drew the sword would die by the sword. He asked him, *"Do you think that I cannot call on my Father, and he will at once put at my disposal more than twelve legions of angels. Shall I not drink the cup the Father has given me and how would the Scriptures be fulfilled that say it must happen in this way?"* (Matthew 26:52-54).

Jesus did not need Peter's help. His violent action had no impact on the arresting party. It just showed his lack of understanding of Jesus' mission. God was in control of the situation, because Jesus had given Him control. His arrest was all part of God's will. As he had submitted to God's will, he allowed himself to be arrested. His betrayal and arrest in this manner fulfilled the Scriptures. Peter was blind to the truth that Jesus was doing God's will and fulfilling the Scriptures. His pride blinded him to Jesus' true purpose and deafened him to his prophecies about his arrest, death and resurrection.

When it came to facing the realities of suffering and death, Jesus and Peter are shown to be equally vulnerable and weak. Peter was deluded about his strength. Jesus faced his vulnerabilities. Peter denied his, as he lacked self-knowledge. He was full of self-confidence at the Last Supper, arguing about who was greatest then boasting he would never abandon Jesus or fall away, and even vowing to go to death with him. Jesus, fully aware of his vulnerabilities confronted his convulsion at the idea of suffering and dying in excruciating pain as he acknowledged his own fragility and fears. Peter, despite his good intentions had no such awareness. As a result, he could not support Jesus and slept as he struggled alone in prayer. Jesus had asked him to keep watch, but he had failed. When Peter did try to support him, his actions were totally out of order.

Peter abandoned Jesus

Then, as Jesus was arrested, Peter, who had said he would go with him even to death fled from the garden. At the first sign of danger to his own skin, he fled. The one who had said he would stand by Jesus, totally abandoned him. Peter fell at the first hurdle. Fortunately, Jesus was not depending on him. He had spent his time in the garden wisely, before his arrest. In a disciplined and meaningful way, he had communicated with his Father as he prepared himself for the pain, suffering and death that lay ahead. Peter spent that time sleeping. He served his human needs, not his spiritual ones. If he had watched and prayed, his human needs would have been met and he would have had the strength to face his ordeals. But he was over-confident his own strength and devotion to Jesus was enough to see him through. How wrong he was! If he had obeyed and watched and prayed, he would have coped when it came to Jesus' betrayal and arrest. He would have had God's strength to cope.

His lack of understanding led him to abandon Jesus, who did not need his help in this situation as he had it totally under his control. Peter failed Jesus when he asked him to pray for him then he abandoned him when he was betrayed and arrested (Mark 14:50). It was all part of God's will. Jesus had to go to the cross alone. He alone was worthy to suffer and die for us. Yet his complete desertion by Peter added to his anguish and sense of aloneness. Despite all his boasting, his frailties had been fully exposed – like the young man who was fully exposed when he fled naked. Peter had boasted he would never fall away, yet, at the first sign of trouble he ran.

Gethsemane reveals Jesus' and Peter's reactions in the time of crisis and Peter fell well short. Jesus faced his frailties, so when he called on God's power he was able to face his ordeal according to God's will. It was a painful, lonely struggle to submit to God's will. Peter denied his own human weakness and believed in his own power to face the crisis, but he was exposed as weak and frail. Those who are vulnerable and open are more receptive to themselves and God. In poverty of spirit and human weakness they cling to God and admit they cannot do it on their own and need God. They know His power begins when their human resourcefulness ends.

Peter followed Jesus at a distance

After Peter abandoned Jesus in Gethsemane, he hid in the darkness outside. Even at that time, he could have lived up to his boasts to stand by Jesus to go with him to prison or even death by returning to the garden to stand with him, but he did not. When he saw Jesus being led away, he followed at a distance (Luke 22:54). His love and loyalty to Jesus was not big enough to admit he had not been true to his word when he fled, but it was strong enough to follow him at a safe distance to the high priest's palace to see what would happen to him. Peter did not follow too closely to be arrested, but far enough away to try to prove his boast to Jesus was true. His pride compelled him to live up to his boasting and would not let him act against it.

Peter was curious to see what would happen to Jesus. Curiosity, not loyalty got the better of him. It was not mixed with conviction. He was acting out of fear. To stand by Jesus would have taken great courage. Following him at a distance then entering the palace courtyard of the high priest put him in a perilous environment. He made his situation worse by not preparing for such a trial. Due to his pride, he had not obeyed Jesus' advice to watch and pray. Now he lacked the strength to stand in the domain of a man determined to condemn and kill Jesus. It was presumptive of him to put himself in the midst of Jesus' enemies. He was blind to his weakness and the leaders' plans. The stage was set for him to commit the worst of sins – to deny Jesus.

Peter denied Jesus the first time

In his desire to prove his love and loyalty for Jesus, Peter was willing to enter the place where he was most at risk – the property of the man determined to kill Jesus. In the courtyard of the high priest's palace, Peter, a Galilean was surrounded with locals from Jerusalem who had been in Gethsemane. His pride and self-confidence stopped wisdom flowing in him. He had not entered the courtyard to stand by Jesus. He could have stood by him when he was arrested, but Peter chose to flee. He could have returned to the garden to stand by Jesus, but hid in the darkness. Then he followed him to the high priest's palace at a distance (not too close, but far enough away). Peter vowed total loyalty to Jesus, but in reality, he showed he was a half-hearted follower as he protected his own skin.

When a servant girl at the gate to the palace courtyard saw Peter in the half light, she believed he was a disciple of Jesus. After he entered the courtyard, he went and warmed himself by the fire with the others. Peter thought more about warming himself and forgot about standing in the light among those who had been in Gethsemane with him. He hoped to go unrecognised. Then the servant girl from the gate moved closer and saw him seated in the firelight. She looked closely at him and said, *"You also were with that Nazarene, Jesus of Galilee!"* But he denied it before them all, *"I don't know or understand what you are talking about!"* he said (Mark 14:66-68).

Events that night revealed Peter's pride and over-confidence in himself and his inability and unwillingness to understand himself. The results of his prayerlessness and independent attitude were revealed throughout that night. He had shown his impulsiveness when he lashed out with his sword in the garden. Then he followed Jesus at a distance into the lion's den of temptation. There, he wanted to avoid recognition as one of Jesus' disciples. For a while, his identity stayed unknown until a servant girl stared at him. When she accused him of being a disciple, he not only failed Jesus, but the disciples as well when he denied any association with him or them.

Peter denied Jesus the second time

After Peter had denied Jesus the first time, he went and stood near the gateway. He moved from the firelight where he was visible to stand in the shadows near the gate where he could make a quick exit. His actions reflected what was happening inside him. His lack of watching and praying that night – his reliance on himself and his own strength moved him away from the Light of the World to the shadows. It was where Peter was spiritually at that moment. Standing near the gate made an easy exit possible. The effect of his lack of prayer was now being revealed. He did not have God's strength to face this trial. He was more in flight-mode than fight-mode. There was still enough confidence in his own ability to stay in the trial – not in the full heat of the fire – but in the cooler air of the shadows. Peter was still relying on his own strength even though he was more in flight-mode. Like his journey from Gethsemane he took the safe option – half in the light and half in the shadows. By standing near the gate, he was trying to stay inconspicuous in the shadows of the courtyard.

Peter had lied about knowing Jesus. Now he was ready to flee. Both actions are far removed from his boasts about his love and loyalty to Jesus. His fear grew when he was accused again of being a disciple. A servant girl saw him and said to those standing there, "*This fellow is one of them!*" They stared at him and asked, "*You aren't one of his disciples too, are you?*" (Matthew 26:71-72). Fearing arrest and even death, Peter lashed out in self-defence, "*I don't know the man!*" And to make his argument more convincing, he added an oath. He was saying, "I swear by God I do not know him." He was now calling God as his witness. A short while ago he did not listen to Him or obey Him. Peter did not keep watch for God and he did not pray to God, but he would use God to save his own skin. He did not even call Jesus by his name. He called him, 'the man,' though he knew he was God's Son. He could not have denied Jesus in a worse way. He relied on his own strength to get through this, but he had not hit rock bottom yet where he would acknowledge his failings and his pride would turn to ashes. He would not have to wait long for that to happen.

Peter denied Jesus the third time

He stayed in his predicament another hour after denying Jesus a second time (Luke 22:59). Those standing by him said, "*Surely you are one of them; your Galilean accent gives you away.*" They knew Jesus and his disciples were Galileans. His accent was the last bit of evidence they needed and it brought him under greater scrutiny. A relative of the man whose ear he had severed, recognised him from the garden. The undeniable truth was out, but he chose to deny it and lie a third time, "*I don't know this man you are talking about!*" And if he was not telling the truth, God could strike him down.

Peter's mouth got him into trouble. It began when he boasted he would not deny Jesus and ended when he denied him a third time. His mouth spoke out of the pride in his heart. He spoke with a Galilean accent to locals from Jerusalem who were Jesus' enemies. Yet the biggest danger to Peter was himself and his mouth, which had denied Jesus. God saw the danger and when it all appeared hopeless He intervened to save Peter from himself and brought him back to himself with the crow of a rooster that marked the end of his fall. As soon as he heard it, he realised he had fulfilled Jesus' words about denying him three times and he wept bitterly (Mark 14:70-72).

In his pride, Peter shamed himself by proving he had lied to Jesus about denying him. He lied about knowing him and would use anyone, even God to get out of trouble. He fell a long way that night. In God's sight, he needed to. He allowed him to fall. With his pride and self-reliance intact, he could not be a faithful servant in His kingdom. After claiming loyalty to Jesus he lost control by calling down curses. Inside Peter was saying, "I am alone and afraid," but he actually said, "I am a liar, I have denied God and refused to do his will." He should have followed Jesus' example: his heart cried out in Gethsemane, "I am alone and afraid, but I am submitting myself fully to God's will."

After Peter had denied Jesus the third time and the rooster crowed, he looked in the Lord's direction only to see Jesus staring back at him. However, it was not a condemnatory look. It was such a look of love. The one he had the hurt most by his denials was looking right at him in total love. Despite all of his boasting, all of his lies, all of his oaths and all of his cursing, Jesus still absolutely loved him. Peter may have denied Jesus, but his Lord was not denying him. It was such a look of love that it broke Peter's heart and he went outside and wept bitterly.

In brokenness, humility and with his strength spent, he repented. With his pride in tatters and his face in the dirt Peter wept. He ended the night where Jesus began his — on his knees, weeping and crying out to God. If Peter had begun his night that way, he would not have ended it on his knees weeping. In humility, he knelt before God broken-hearted. Only in that condition of humility and brokenness, could he be useful in His kingdom and lead Jesus' Church.

Peter failed big time. He had boasted he would stand by Jesus and die with him. He was asked to keep watch whilst Jesus prayed, but he fell asleep three times. He cut off a man's ear then abandoned Jesus when he was arrested. Then he cursed and denied him three times. When the rooster crowed, he recalled Jesus' prophecy about denying him. To his self-reliance and pride, that rooster crow was like the trumpet blast to Jericho's walls — they came tumbling down. Those in Jericho trusted in their walls for safety, he trusted in his own love and loyalty to Jesus. Peter trusted in himself to get him through his trials that night. He had to learn he was weak, helpless and fallible and trust in God's love for him and His loyalty to him.

That night, Peter lied and denied his identity as Jesus' disciple. He was unwilling to face the consequences for confessing his true identity and speaking the truth as Jesus had done to Caiaphas. He lied with an oath to avoid suffering, but it did not stop him suffering. Realising he had fulfilled Jesus' prophecy about denying him broke Peter. Jesus' pain and suffering were inflicted by others. Peter's pain and suffering were self-inflicted. He clung to his life and risked losing everything that gave it meaning. He acted against his best desires and how he saw himself. Jesus told him his spirit was willing but his flesh was weak. He experienced it when he slept instead of praying. Without prayer he lacked power to endure his trials. He dealt with the accusations in his own strength and failed. He would have received God's power only by acknowledging his vulnerabilities and knowing his human weaknesses.

Only God's power could have enabled Peter to overcome his natural tendency to save his own skin at the cost of what he believed and to be strong in his identity as Jesus' disciple regardless of the cost. But he trusted in his own courage. The power God gives endures suffering. It identifies itself with all who suffer. Peter stands for human weakness, which lacks self-knowledge and knowledge of God and the power of God and the power of prayer to tap into the power of God. His self-inflicted suffering achieved nothing for others. Jesus' suffering was God ordained and achieved everything on behalf of sinful man.

Despite Peter's failings that night, God showed him abundant grace on Resurrection Day. When the women went to the tomb to anoint Jesus' body, they found it empty. Angels appeared and told them to tell the disciples '**and Peter**' Jesus had risen (Mark 16:7). Despite his pride, boasting, denials, cursing and swearing, Peter was still on God's heart. He gave Peter a special mention that day. What grace! More grace was shown to Peter when Jesus appeared to him that day to restore him (Luke 24:34). He had to wait two more weeks before his ministry was restored when Jesus provided him with a miraculous catch of fish on the Sea of Galilee (John 21:1-23). Peter failed and he failed big time in Jesus' final hours. However, God's kingdom is a kingdom of restoration. After he failed, God restored him. What a God! It shows no matter how much we fail in life or mess up, restoration is always available if we, like Peter humble ourselves and repent.

John, the disciple whom Jesus loved

After being with Jesus for over three years – hearing his words; seeing his miracles and his interactions with people so affected John, he called himself, 'the disciple Jesus loved'. Not once, but five times: John 13:23; John 19:26; John 20:2; John 21:7 and John 21:20. He may not have seen Jesus was fully God and fully man or known the dynamics of God's kingdom or why he had come to Earth. One thing he knew was, Jesus loved him. He lived in a state of being loved by him. He based his identity on being loved by him – what a way to live! When Jesus said he would be betrayed, John leaned back against him to ask who it was. From the way they were laying, he would have pressed his head into Jesus' chest. It shows such intimacy could be experienced only by someone who knew they were loved by the Son of God who is God.

John did not reciprocate that love in Gethsemane when he fell asleep three times after Jesus asked him to keep watch or when he deserted him as he was arrested (Mark 14:32-42). Yet, he was different to Peter. He trusted in Jesus' love for him. Peter trusted in his love for Jesus. There is a big difference between the two. Peter trusted in his own love and loyalty to Jesus and it came crashing down that night when he ended it by cursing and denying him three times. John trusted in Jesus' love for him and he was able to face the trial of going into the high priest's presence and to witness Jesus' crucifixion at Calvary. Out of his love and loyalty for John, he entrusted the one he loved to look after his mother (John 19:25-27).

It was John's trust in Jesus' love for him that enabled him, not Peter (who had trusted in his own love, which resulted in him denying Jesus) that saw it was Jesus in his resurrected form that provided the miracle catch of fish on the Sea of Galilee (John 21:7). He saw what Peter could not see. Like John, when we see Jesus' love for us, we see things clearly and receive all things freely. It is why Jesus chose John to look after Mary (John 19:25-27). He was the disciple most like himself. John was so enamoured by Jesus' love; he could not keep away from him. He even followed him as he reinstated Peter in his ministry (John 21:15-23). It is the mark of a true disciple, who knows they are loved by Jesus and follows him wherever he goes.

Judas Iscariot

Judas is first mentioned in the Gospels when Jesus chose him to be an apostle. Mark 3:19 and Luke 6:16 refer to him as a betrayer or traitor. He is introduced for what he is best remembered for – betraying Jesus. Judas would have seen Jesus' miracles and heard his teachings and may not have known who he was, where he was from or understood the dynamics of his kingdom, but he would have seen the constancy of his selfless love, compassion, patience and kindness for three years. Yet all he witnessed did not effect his hard heart, which was seen when he berated Mary for anointing Jesus with valuable perfume to prepare him for his burial (John 12:1-8).

John 12:6 says Judas was a thief. Jesus entrusted him to look after his money, but he helped himself to it. In Jesus, all the resources of God's kingdom were available to Judas, yet he chose to steal pennies from his purse. How sad! All that Judas had seen or not seen in Jesus over three years was reinforced by Jesus' response to his anointing by Mary. It made Jesus betray him (Matthew 26:14-16). Again Judas' small-mindedness and hard-heartedness let him settle for small change – thirty pieces of silver. Luke 22:3-6 says Satan entered Judas before he betrayed Jesus, who had so hardened his heart; the Devil could enter him to do his bidding to get Jesus killed. In Jesus, God would have opened up the abundant resources of his kingdom to Judas if he had waited twenty-four hours until Jesus died for his sins on the cross of Calvary. If Judas had been the only man on Earth at that time, he would have still died for him.

He was not only a thief and a betrayer, but he was also a liar too. At the Last Supper, when Jesus said one of the Twelve would betray him, he said, *"Surely not I Rabbi!"* But Jesus said, *"You yourself have said it"* (Matthew 26:21-25). After Judas was identified as his betrayer, he went out and it was night (John 13:30). Interestingly, after Satan entered Judas all his actions took place at night: he complained about the waste of money when Mary anointed Jesus; at the Last Supper, he lied to Jesus that he was not his betrayer; then he betrayed him to the chief priests before leading them to Gethsemane; and identified Jesus by kissing him. This sign of friendship (a kiss) in the darkness was the last time Jesus saw Judas.

Only in the light of the following day did Judas see the light – the result of his actions. When he saw the Sanhedrin had condemned Jesus, he was filled with remorse and returned the money to the priests at the temple, saying he had shed innocent blood. They were not interested and told him it was his problem. Judas threw the coins into the temple then went and hung himself (Matthew 27:1-10). Even in death he messed up. He tried to make amends himself and pay for his own sins by killing himself. If he had waited for just a few hours, Jesus' death would have paid for his sins.

After seeing Jesus was condemned, he was remorseful, not repentant. After denying Jesus three times, Peter wept in true repentance. Jesus forgave him then restored him and his ministry, filled him with the Spirit and let him lead his Church. If Judas had truly repented and not tried to make amends himself, he would have been forgiven. What he had done made him angry with himself. He sought a human solution by returning the money then he tried to wipe out his sin by paying the price with his own life.

Women from Galilee

Jesus' great love for women was seen as he carried his cross to Calvary (Luke 23:27-31). Despite the pain of his flogging and carrying a cross, he was more concerned about the plight of the women following him than he was about his own. Out of selfless love, Jesus reassured them. Whilst hanging on the cross in excruciating pain, he showed the same love when he placed Mary into the care of his disciple John (John 19:25-27). His love for women did not end after he died. Matthew 28:8-10 says they were the first to see Jesus after he rose from the dead. John 20:10-18 says Mary Magdalene was the first to see risen Jesus. Jesus honoured Mary and her love by delaying his return to his heavenly Father to appear to her – such love! Mary and the other women stayed with Jesus to the end. They supported him during his ministry as they travelled around Israel with him. They were present at Calvary and saw Jesus hang in excruciating pain for six hours on the cross. They witnessed his death then watched Joseph of Arimathea and Nicodemus bury him in the tomb (Luke 23:49-55). The women's loyalty and faithfulness were repaid when they were the first ones to see Jesus after he rose from the dead. In Jesus' eyes, the women were worthy to see him first.

Annas

Jesus was tried first by Annas, who had been high priest in Israel. The Romans deposed him in 15AD and made his son in law, Caiaphas high priest instead. The Jews saw the role as a lifelong appointment and still revered Annas. He tried to get Jesus to testify about himself by asking him about his teaching and his disciples. He said he had spoken openly and Annas should ask those who had heard him as they knew what he had said. Jesus was telling him he should do the right thing and produce witnesses if he had a legitimate charge against him and for this trial to be legitimate. Annas was taking judicial short cuts as he tried to make Jesus bear witness against himself, but he was rebuffed by Jesus. As high priest, he should have known and behaved better and followed judicial procedure rather than make Jesus testify against himself. Jesus was having none of it and called him to task. He rebuked him without fear and the high priest was humiliated as he was given a short, sharp lecture in correct legal procedure. Then an official struck Jesus in the face. It was a cowardly act to strike a bound man and unjust to treat the accused as a convicted criminal. Jesus looked to Annas to reprove such an aggressive act, but he did not (John 18:19-24).

Jesus' humble reaction to this violence was a rebuke to the one who struck him and to Annas who had allowed it then let it go unpunished. When he realised his line of inquiry was going nowhere and Jesus, who showed no fear of him was making him look bad, he sent him to be tried by Caiaphas. Annas read no charges to him, produced no witnesses or evidence against him and interrogated Jesus himself. By asking Jesus about his teaching and his disciples, he hoped to hear something in his teaching that would result in a religious or political charge against him. Annas was willing to take any measures necessary – legal or illegal to get Jesus to incriminate himself. He would have condemned Jesus next day and took him to Pilate to be tried by him. Along with other religious leaders, he would have falsely accused him at his trials before Pilate and Herod (Luke 23:1-10). He achieved his goal of having Jesus sentenced to death, but even then it was not enough for him. As God's Son bled and died on the cross, he heaped scorn on him. Not once did he consider the possibility, Jesus had told the truth when he said he was the Christ, God's Son.

Caiaphas and the Sanhedrin

Caiaphas was Israel's high priest. The Sanhedrin was the religious and legal body that governed the Jews, even under Roman rule. It consisted of seventy men and the high priest. It needed twenty-five members to be present to carry out its business lawfully and only in daytime. Those gathered that night, like Caiaphas, wanted to kill Jesus. They had false witnesses testify against him in order to find a charge against him, but their testimonies did not agree. Caiaphas wanted Jesus to answer the charges, hoping he would incriminate himself, but he stayed silent (Mark 14:55-59). In order to draw an admission from Jesus that would condemn him, he asked him to swear by God if he was the Christ. Such a confession would result in a charge of blasphemy. It was the charge Jesus was accused of when he said he was the Christ. The leaders agreed he was guilty and worthy of death. None of them stopped to think if what Jesus had said was true. The verdict did not relieve their hatred. Without decency or self-respect, they spat on Jesus and struck him (Matthew 26:63-66).

They sentenced Jesus at dawn, though there was meant to be a day between convicting and sentencing. He was taken to Pilate. With trumped up charges and lies they hoped to persuade him to condemn Jesus. They said he was a political revolutionary threatening Rome's government and had said paying taxes to Caesar was illegal. Being a bad religious influence and not paying taxes would not convince Pilate to condemn him – most Jews avoided paying taxes. Then they claimed Jesus had said he was a king, which meant he was a threat to Rome. If Pilate released him, he would face serious repercussions from Rome. He tried to bypass the leaders and put Jesus' fate in the hands of the crowd that was there, but the leaders stirred them up to have Barabbas released and Jesus crucified (Mark 15:1-15).

These religious leaders were not content with having their way. Seeing Jesus nailed to the cross was not enough for them. They mocked him (Mark 15:31-32). The ones who had been appointed to rule over the people of God with truth, justice, uprightness, integrity, honesty and without bias had failed in every way. Out of hypocrisy, envy and unbelief, the Jewish leaders had rejected Jesus; God's Messiah and treated him with cruelty and contempt.

Pilate

Pontius Pilate was Roman procurator in Judea from 26AD to 37AD. He was in charge of the Roman army that occupied Judea. It was based in Caesarea, with a small detachment in Jerusalem. As the authority in Judea, he could ratify or reverse any decisions made by the Sanhedrin, the ruling body of the Jews. Pilate sought to always please Emperor Tiberius, by ensuring peace in Judea at all costs, even quelling any signs of rebellion at the cost of justice.

When the Jewish leaders brought Jesus to be tried by Pilate, it was a problem he did not need. He told them to try Jesus themselves, but they refused. They wanted him to try Jesus and execute him. They believed their charges against him would persuade Pilate to condemn him – but he saw through them. They implied Jesus was a threat to the Roman Empire, but after questioning him, he was convinced he posed no such threat. When they said he claimed to be a king, Pilate took this charge seriously. If Tiberius learned he had released a king – a threat to the Empire, Pilate would be in trouble. He did not care if Jesus was a king but asked out of curiosity. He knew he had done something so bad to upset the leaders, they had handed him over to be killed by a non-Jew at their Passover. Jesus reassured him his kingship was no threat to Rome as it was not of this world. Then he told Pilate he was the king of truth – the God of reality. Truth can be found only in the person of Jesus.

Throughout Jesus' trial, Pilate passed the buck, but it kept returning to him. He knew Jesus was innocent. He had tried to pass it back to the Jewish leaders when he told them to try him themselves, but they were having none of it. When he learned he was a Galilean, Pilate passed the buck to Herod, the ruler of Galilee. He hoped Herod would make the decision for him, but that did not happen. Pilate was in a place he did not want to be with a problem he could do without. If he did not condemn an innocent man, these leaders would report him to Tiberius for releasing a man who claimed to be a king. Any king was a threat in the eyes of the ruler of the Empire. To escape his dilemma, Pilate passed the buck once again – this time to the crowd gathered outside the Antonia Fortress that day to ask him to practise his Passover custom of releasing one of his prisoners to them.

Pilate had a custom at Passover of releasing a prisoner. He put Jesus forward as one of two to be released. He thought the crowd would choose him, not Barabbas, a murderer. His plan failed when the Jewish leaders stirred up the crowd to call for Barabbas to be released and for Jesus to be condemned. Determined to have him released, Pilate adopted a new strategy. He had Jesus flogged, hoping that when the crowd saw him, they would be satisfied he had been punished enough and would not demand his death.

He saw through the rulers' accusations. Jesus was innocent in his mind and his wife confirmed it after having a dream (Matthew 27:19), but Pilate was too weak to see justice done. He had Jesus flogged and presented him to the crowd dressed in a purple (kingly) robe. He looked anything but a king and Pilate rightly said, "*Here is the man! Here is your king*!" The sight did not invoke pity in the crowd as he had hoped. The Jewish leaders prompted them to call for Barabbas to be freed and for Jesus to be crucified. After this plan to have him released failed, Pilate told the leaders to crucify him themselves as he found him innocent. They said that under their law he must die for claiming to be God's Son. Pilate asked Jesus where he was from, but he did not reply. When he said he had power to free or crucify him, Jesus said it was only because God had given it to him. Pilate was not in control, God was. Jesus added, the leaders were more guilty of sin than him as they had offered him up. In response to this kindness Pilate tried to get Jesus freed.

Pilate asked the crowd again who he should free and received the same answer. When he saw he was getting nowhere, but a riot was starting, he washed his hands, saying he was innocent of Jesus' blood. Then he handed him over to be crucified (Luke 23:13-25). Pilate knew he was innocent. He was the only champion Jesus had during this ordeal, but he was a weak champion. When it came to saving Jesus' neck or his own, he saved his own. Washing his hands was a picture of what he had been trying to achieve in this trial. Jesus' situation was a problem he could do without. When it appeared a riot would break out, Pilate had a choice – hand over an innocent man to be crucified or face a riot – the news of which could reach Rome and he could lose his position. He made the choice in a moment, but his decision would have consequences for all eternity.

Herod

Herod Antipas was the son of King Herod the Great, who ruled at the time Jesus was born. He and his son ruled Galilee in Israel for the Romans. Herod Antipas may not have known much about Jesus, but the Lord certainly knew a lot about him. He may not have been aware of it, but there was a historical legacy between them. He may have forgotten that about thirty years earlier his Father had ordered Jesus' death shortly after his birth when he decreed all boys born in Bethlehem, aged two or under to be killed (Matthew 2:1-18). After Jesus' baptism and temptation and before his Galilean ministry began, Herod Antipas imprisoned Jesus' cousin, John the Baptist and two years later he had him beheaded (Mark 6:14-28).

During Jesus' trial by Pilate, the Roman governor learned that he was a Galilean. As Herod was the ruler of Galilee, Pilate sent Jesus to Herod to be tried by him. Herod had heard about Jesus and his miracles and for a long time had hoped to see him. When Jesus appeared before him, he hoped he would perform a miracle for him. However, Jesus did not perform any signs or wonders, nor did he answer any of Herod's questions or respond to any of the Jewish leaders' accusations. Herod did not like his power being ignored. It bothered him that Jesus was not threatened by his power and presence, so he resorted to mocking and ridiculing him. Herod put pleasure and entertainment above justice.

Herod was more concerned about having fun than seeing Jesus had a fair trial. He wanted Jesus to entertain him, like a performer doing a magic show. Despite his pressing and the accusations against him, he stood before Herod in quiet dignity. Jesus' silence made the situation awkward for Herod. It provoked him and his soldiers to mock Jesus. After getting some form of cheap entertainment from Jesus, Herod dressed him in a purple robe and sent him back to Pilate. Pilate had sent him a man claiming to be the king of the Jews, so Herod dressed Jesus in a royal robe of purple and sent him back to the Roman governor dressed like a king. Herod was pleased Pilate had sent Jesus to be tried by him and the pair became friends – before then, they had been enemies.

The two dying criminals

The felons insulted Jesus (Mark 15:32) from the time he was crucified until one of them had a change of heart. It seems he saw and heard something on the cross that revealed Jesus was the Christ, God's Son. He had seen the sign, saying Jesus was the king of the Jews. He had heard Jesus' words and the insults hurled at him and thought about them, unlike the other felon who turned on him. Instead of cursing and reviling his executioners and onlookers, he mocked, *"Aren't you the Christ? Save yourself!"* As an afterthought he added, *"and us!"* (Luke 23:39), but Jesus ignored him totally.

The other felon rebuked him, *"Don't you fear God, seeing you are under the same sentence."* He was saying, "You may not fear God, but you'll be facing Him soon. In view of your imminent death and judgment you might at least fear Him and not incur guilt for reviling this fellow victim." He added, *"We are being punished justly, for we are receiving what our deeds deserved, but he has done nothing wrong."* (Luke 23:40-41). The man had led a sinful life until justice overtook him. Now he was nailed to a cross and dying. Instead of mocking Jesus, he opened to the idea he might be who he said he was and whom the others had mocked him for being, the Christ. He confessed his sins and accepted his suffering as a just punishment for his wickedness. After proclaiming Jesus' innocence, he declared his belief in his divinity when he asked, *"Jesus, remember me when you come into your kingdom!"* (Luke 23:42).

Pilate's sign on his cross read, 'The king of the Jews' (Mark 15:26). It would have informed this dying thief of the charge against Jesus. He would have heard the passers-by, the leaders and soldiers insult him and seen he did not respond. He had heard the leaders call him the king of the Jews and the Son of God. He had heard Jesus call God, 'Father' and ask him to forgive his executioners before he entrusted his mother to his disciple's care. All this thief saw and heard helped him to repent, that is, change his mind. He changed it from believing that the man dying next to him was a criminal being punished justly for his crimes to believing he was innocent and suffering unjustly and that he was the Christ, the Son of God.

Whatever he saw or heard made him take his mind off his own pain and fix it on Jesus. It would have been such a painful ordeal for him to speak. He would have pushed down on the nails in his feet to inhale, in order to speak. It would have intensified the pain shooting through his body. Yet he believed it was worth it to speak to Jesus. He did not ask much of Jesus and asked it in such a way, it left the outcome to him. He asked simply that he should remember him when he came in his kingdom. With his newfound faith in Christ, he ignored his present pain and suffering to focus on his future. He believed Jesus was the Christ who would return in glory with his Messianic kingdom. When he looked at Jesus now, he saw a man who on all appearances was condemned as a criminal by his people and the Roman authorities dying on a cross, reviled and mocked by all but a few. Yet, this dying thief professed his belief Jesus was the Christ, God's Son, who was God and begged him to remember him when he returned in glory. Jesus rewarded his faith by saying, "*Today, you will be with me in paradise!*" (Luke 23:43).

Jesus' words show we are not saved by being perfect or by obeying religious rituals. Salvation is received through a humble, penitent heart that needs forgiveness and acknowledges Jesus is God's Son and is God. '*Today*' shows Jesus' salvation is immediate and present. There was no delay between his response to the thief's request. For him, salvation was there to be taken, there and then. If he had waited, he would have missed it. He did not. He was losing his physical life, but he gained eternal life. The felon shows us how to be saved. He realised who he was: a sinner and who Jesus was, the Christ, God's Son. Jesus did not condemn him for his sins, but blessed him with eternal life – no matter how much he had messed up.

He accepted Jesus' offer of eternal life. The other felon did not. The unrepentant sinner refused to submit to Jesus and insulted him instead. He did ask Jesus to save him, but his heart was not in the request. He mockingly told Jesus, "*Save yourself, if you are the Christ!*" Then he added, almost as an afterthought, "and whilst you are saving yourself, save us!" It was a selfish plea from an unrepentant heart. As Jesus did not answer him, he died unsaved. He showed no fear of God during his ordeal or any remorse for his sin. Though suffering and dying, he stayed defiant to the end.

The centurion

When he died, the centurion called him the Son of God (Mark 15:39). He would have seen many die from crucifixion, but never in the way Jesus died. He would have noticed he did not curse during his painful ordeal and heard him call God, 'his Father' as he forgave his killers. He would have heard Jesus entrust his mother into his disciple's care before granting salvation to a dying felon. He would have seen him bow his head as he gave up his spirit – not throwing it back to gasp a final breath like all victims of crucifixion. He would have seen darkness fall, felt the ground shake and seen the rocks split before reasoning Jesus' death was the cause of it all.

His words reveal the power of the cross. It shows Jesus' death opened the door to salvation and an ongoing relationship between God and man, to Jews and non-Jews. A soldier is an unexpected source for such a declaration. He saw Jesus as God's Son by the way he died. He died feeling God-forsaken. He saw him as God's Son. He died experiencing God's absence, but his death revealed God's presence to this soldier. One felt God's absence, the other His presence. The cross is a symbol of the absence and the presence of God. He is present in conditions that speak most powerfully and tragically of His absence. In Jesus' suffering, God identifies with our suffering and becomes one with us.

Joseph of Arimathea

Joseph was a secret follower of Jesus and a member of the Sanhedrin. It is not clear if he was at the meeting where Jesus was condemned. If he was, then he did not speak out for him. However, after Jesus' death, he asked Pilate for his dead body. The disciples who had followed him publicly had deserted him. This leader who had followed him secretly, boldly came forward and did the right thing. He risked his reputation as a leader to give Jesus a proper burial. The disciples, who had boldly declared they would never desert him and would stand with him even in death had fled. Joseph who had previously hidden his allegiance to Jesus boldly took a stand that could cost him dearly. He was willing to pay the price to bury Jesus – a price his disciples had been unwilling to pay.

Prophecies fulfilled in the Passion

Jesus' death on the cross had been planned by God before the world was created in order to redeem mankind from sin and restore us to an on-going relationship with God that would last forever. Throughout the Scriptures God foretold the Christ would die for our sins to redeem us from sin and death. Jesus fulfilled many prophecies in his final hours:

Psalm 41:9 predicted Jesus' betrayal: *'Even my close friend whom I trusted, he who shared my bread, has lifted up his heel against me.'* He predicted this at the Last Supper (John 13:21-30) and it was fulfilled in Gethsemane (Mark 14:43-45). Zechariah 11:12 reveals the price Judas received for betraying him: *'thirty pieces of silver.'* Zechariah 13:7 foretold the Eleven deserting him: *'Strike the shepherd and the sheep will be scattered.'* His arrest fulfilled Isaiah 53:8: *'By oppression and judgment he was taken away.'* His silence at his trials (Mark 14:61 and Mark 15:5) fulfilled Isaiah 53:7, *'As a sheep before the shearers is silent, so he did not open his mouth.'* When Judas returned the money, the priests, used it to buy the potter's field (Matthew 27:3-10), it fulfilled Zechariah 11:12-13, *'They paid me thirty pieces of silver. And the Lord said to me, "Throw it to the potter" – the handsome price at which they priced me. So I took the thirty pieces of silver and threw them into the house of the Lord to the potter.'*

Isaiah 52:13-15 says Christ's appearance would be disfigured beyond that of any man and his form marred beyond human likeness. Then Isaiah 50:6 says, *'I offered my back to those who beat me, my cheeks to those who pulled out my beard; I did not hide my face from mocking and spitting.'* After the leaders condemned Jesus, they spat in his face and hit him. They blindfolded him then hit him and demanded he say who hit him. Others slapped him then put him under guard. The guards beat him and blindfolded him. They struck him and demanded he prophesy who had hit him (Mark 14:65 and Luke 22:63-65). Pilate had him flogged. Soldiers pressed a crown of thorns on his head. They spat on him and mocked him then struck him repeatedly on the head with a wooden staff. With his face swollen and bruised and his skin ripped apart and the raw flesh exposed by the flogging, he carried the cross on his bleeding shoulder to Calvary (Mark 15:15-20).

Prophecies fulfilled by Jesus' crucifixion

Before creating the world, God determined Jesus would die on a cross for the sins of the world: '*He was pierced for our transgressions, he was crushed for our iniquities, the punishment that brought us peace was upon him and by his wounds we are healed. We all like sheep have gone astray, each of us has turned to his own way, and God has laid on him the iniquity of us all. Yet it was God's will to crush him and cause him to suffer and though God makes his life a guilt offering, he will see his offspring and prolong his days and the will of God will prosper in his hand. So I will give him a portion among the great and he will divide the spoils among the strong, because he poured out his life unto death and was numbered with the sinners. For he bore the sins of many and made intercession for the sinners.*' (Isaiah 53:3-12). Jesus fulfilled all this by dying on a cross.

Psalm 22:16 says a band of evil men have encircled me and have pierced my hands and feet. This was fulfilled when Jesus was nailed to the cross. He was crucified between two felons (Mark 15:27-28). It fulfilled Isaiah 53:12, which says he would be counted with the lawless ones. Psalm 22:18 says, '*they divided my garments among them and cast lots for my clothing.*' This was fulfilled as Jesus hung on the cross when the four soldiers each took an item of his clothing then cast lots to see who would get his undergarment (John 19:23-24).

Psalm 22:7-8 says '*All who see me mock me; they hurl insults at me, shaking their heads. "He trusts in the Lord. Let the Lord rescue him. Let him deliver him, since he delights in him."*' These words were fulfilled when passers-by insulted Jesus, shook their heads and said, "*So, you who are going to destroy the temple and build it in three days, come down from the cross and save yourself!*" The leaders mocked him too, '"*He saved others," they said, "but can't save himself!" Let this Christ, this King of Israel, come down now from the cross, that we may see and believe*'" (Mark 15:29-32). The soldiers mocked him, saying, "*If you are the king of the Jews, save yourself.*" One felon mocked him, "*Aren't you the Christ? Save yourself and us!*" (Luke 23:36-39). They wanted him to come down from the cross to prove he was the Christ. He was the only one who wanted to stay there. By seeing his crucifixion to the end, he saved us completely.

Prophecies fulfilled by Jesus' death and burial

When Jesus took on our sin and God poured out his wrath against sin on him, just before he died he cried, *"My God, my God, why have you forsaken me?"* fulfilling the words of Psalm 22:1. He said this so we will never have to. Psalm 22:14-15 says, *'I am poured out like water and all my bones are out of joint. My heart has turned to wax. It has melted away within me. My strength is dried up like a potsherd, and my tongue sticks to the roof of my mouth, you lay me in the dust of death.'* When Jesus said, *"I thirst,"* he was offered vinegar to drink (John 19:28-29), fulfilling the words of Psalm 69:21: *'They put gall in my food and gave me vinegar for my thirst.'* Then he died.

When Pilate's soldiers found Jesus was dead they did not break his legs. It fulfilled Exodus 12:46: *'Not one of the bones of the Passover Lamb must be broken,'* and Psalm 34:20 which says, *'He protects all his bones, not one of them will be broken.'* When a soldier pierced his side (John 19:31-34) it fulfilled Zechariah 12:10, *'They will look on me, the one they have pierced.'* Isaiah 53:9 says, *'he was assigned a grave with the wicked and rich.'* Jesus died like a criminal but was buried in the tomb of wealthy Joseph of Arimathea (Luke 23:50-53).

Jesus' suffering and death reveal God and His love

On the cross, we see **love** – God's love poured out for us in giving His Son to pay the price for all our sins. We see **sacrifice** – as the God of creation willingly died for our sins. We see **humility** – as God humbled himself and became a man to die on a cross to pay the price for our sins to redeem sinful man from sin, sickness, disease and death. We see **selflessness** – Jesus had no thought for himself during this excruciatingly painful ordeal. We see **obedience** – Jesus obediently, submitted to his Father's will and bled and died for our sins. We see **wisdom** – supreme wisdom that turned the worst thing that has ever happened in the world into the best thing that has ever happened. We see **grace** – the abundant grace of God's Son dying in our place – the innocent dying for the guilty – the pure dying for the impure – the sinless dying for the sinful – the most perfect person dying for imperfect people. We see **mercy** – God could have wiped us out for our sin, but in His mercy, he sent his Son to die in our place. What a wonderful loving God and what a wonderful Saviour is Jesus!

Appendix 1

Establishing a chronology of events

To find the chronology of events of Jesus' final twenty-four hours, first it is necessary to find the order in which they happened. Once the order of events has been established, the timing for each of the events will be examined. The events of Jesus' final hours happened in six different stages, as shown below:

Events of Jesus' final hours

1. The Last Supper
2. The Garden of Gethsemane
3. Jesus' trials and Peter's denials
4. Jesus' trials by Pilate and Herod
5. The Crucifixion
6. Jesus' burial

The events of Jesus' final hours began when he and his disciples arrived at the Upper Room in Jerusalem for the Last Supper.

Order and timing of events at the Last Supper

Let's look at the Gospel record of events that happened at the Last Supper to see what it reveals about their order and their timing:

Mt 26:20-30	Mk 14:17-26	Lk 22:14-38	Jn 13:1-17:26
Arrival at house	Arrival at house	Arrival at house	Arrival at house
Meal began	Meal began	Wine served	Feet washed
Judas' betrayal	Judas' betrayal	New Covenant	Meal began
New Covenant	New Covenant	Bread broken	Judas' betrayal
Bread broken	Bread broken	Meal ended	Judas left house
Wine served	Wine served	Wine served	Peter's denials
Meal ended	Meal ended	Judas' betrayal	"I am the way…"
Hymn sung	Hymn sung	Disciples rowed	Spirit promised
		Peter's denials	"I am the Vine!"
		Swords found	Hatred of world
			Holy Spirit's work
			Jesus prayed

Order and timing of events at the Last Supper

Jesus arrived at the house as evening came (Mark 14:17). Evenings begin at sunset. The Jerusalem solar calendar says it sets at Passover this year at 18:20 Hours[b]. The time it sets is unchanged over time. If it sets at that time today, it would have set at 18:20 Hours that day. He would have arrived at the house after then. In Bible times, feet were washed upon entering a home, so the first event that night was washing his disciples' feet. Luke 22:14 says, *'when the hour came,'* he said, *"I have eagerly desired to eat this Passover with you before I suffer."* His words show the Last Supper was a Passover meal. It began at dusk (Numbers 9:3). Dusk falls about half an hour after sunset or 18:50 Hours. If he arrived at 18:20 Hours, he would have washed their feet from then until 18:50 Hours when the meal began. And the order of events of a Passover meal will set events at the Last Supper in the correct chronology.

Order of events at a Passover meal

1. A prayer of blessing is said
2. **First cup of wine is served*** (Luke 22:17-18)
3. Hands are washed for the first time
4. Bitter herbs are eaten
5. Bread is broken and eaten
6. The Passover story is told
7. Second cup of wine is served
8. Hands are washed for the second time
9. Bread is blessed and eaten
10. Bitter herbs are eaten
11. **The host makes a sop (sandwich)*** (John 13:26)
12. The Passover meal is eaten
13. **Bread is eaten*** (Mark 14:22 and Luke 22:19)
14. **Thanks is given*** (Mark 14:22 and Luke 22:19)
15. **Third cup of wine is served*** (Mark 14:23 and Luke 22:20)
16. Hallel recited
17. Fourth cup of wine is served
18. **A hymn is sung*** (Matthew 26:30 and Mark 14:26)
19. **A final prayer*** (John 17:1-26)

*Events at a traditional Passover that took place at the Last Supper

First cup of wine is served

After saying he had desired to eat the meal with his disciples, he took wine, gave thanks and gave it them, saying he would not drink it again until God's kingdom came. At a Passover meal, the first of four cups of wine is served as the meal begins. If Luke 22:15-18 recorded the first cup being served, it was the next event at the Last Supper and occurred at 18:50 Hours as the meal began.

Host makes a sop (sandwich)

At a usual Passover meal, the second cup of wine was served after the host told the original Passover story and before he made a sandwich (sop) of the lamb as the main meal began. Mark 14:18-21 says Jesus predicted his betrayal as they ate. He identified Judas as his betrayer by handing him the sop he was holding then Judas left the house and it was night (John 13:25-30). Night falls about thirty minutes after dusk. If dusk fell that day at 18:50 Hours, night would have fallen at 19:20 Hours. He would have predicted his betrayal after that time. It would have been the third event that night. John 13:31-38 and Luke 22:31-34 then say Jesus predicted Peter's denials, but Luke says it was after the meal. Matthew 26:20-25 and Mark 14:18-21 agree that Jesus predicted his betrayal as they ate. As John then says he foretold Peter's denials, it would make it the fourth event to occur that night. Jesus predicted his denials again that night on the way to Gethsemane (Matthew 26:31-35 and Mark 14:27-31).

Bread is eaten and the third cup of wine is served

After predicting his betrayal; John 13:31-38 says Jesus predicted Peter's denials. Luke 22:31-34 agrees but says his disciples argued over greatness between the two predictions. Luke recorded these events after the meal, but they would have taken place as they ate. It was a style of his writing and not a chronological discrepancy. These fourth and fifth events that night occurred before Jesus instituted the New Covenant (Mark 14:22-25). He took bread, gave thanks then broke it and gave it to his disciples saying it was his body broken for them. Then he took the wine, gave thanks and gave it to them saying it was his blood poured out for the forgiveness of sins. At a traditional meal, the third cup of wine was served after the host made the sop. It implies Jesus served this cup as he instituted the New Covenant.

A hymn is sung and a prayer is offered

After instituting the New Covenant, Matthew 26:30 and Mark 14:26 say they sang a hymn then left the house. Luke 22:35-38 says his disciples found two swords before they left. John 17:1-26 says Jesus prayed for himself, his disciples and for all believers before leaving. At a traditional meal, a hymn is sung after the fourth cup of wine is served and before a final prayer is made. If they followed that order of events, they would have sung a hymn before he prayed. Finding swords would have been the last event before they left.

Before Jesus prayed and his disciples found swords, John 14:1-16:33 says he told them he was the way, the truth and the life. Then Jesus promised to send them the Holy Spirit to be with them forever. Next he said he was the True Vine before telling them the world would hate them because it had hated him. Then Jesus taught his disciples about the Spirit before he prayed for himself, his disciples and for all believers. Jesus would have taught all these things after they sang a hymn and before they found two swords and left for Gethsemane. It would mean the order of events of the Last Supper is as follows:

Order of events at the Last Supper

- Jesus arrived at the Upper Room in Jerusalem (Mark 14:17)
- Jesus washed his disciples' feet (John 13:1-17)
- The Passover meal began (Luke 22:14-16)
- Betrayal predicted (Matthew 26:20-25 and Mark 14:18-21)
- The disciples argued over who was greatest (Luke 22:24-30)
- Peter's denials predicted (Luke 22:31-34 and John 13:31-38)
- The New Covenant (Matthew 26:26-29 and Mark 14:22-25)
- Jesus sang a hymn (Matthew 26:30 and Mark 14:26)
- Jesus said, "I am the way the truth and the life (John 14:1-14)
- Jesus promised the Holy Spirit (John 14:15-33)
- Jesus said, "I am the true vine" (John 15:1-17)
- He said the world would hate his disciples (John 15:18-16:4)
- Jesus taught on the work of the Holy Spirit (John 16:5-31)
- Jesus prayed (John 17:1-26)
- Jesus' disciples found two swords (Luke 22:35-38)

Order and timing of events in Gethsemane

Let's look at events that happened in Gethsemane as recorded in the Gospel to see what they reveal about their order and timing:

Matt 26:30-56	Mark 14:26-52	Luke 22:39-54	John 18:1-12
Walk to garden	Walk to garden	Walk to garden	Walk to garden
Peter's denials	Peter's denials	Eleven to pray	Jesus betrayed
Peter to watch	Peter to watch	Jesus prayed	Man's ear cut
First prayer	First prayer	Angelic visit	Jesus arrested
Second prayer	Second prayer	Jesus betrayed	
Third prayer	Third prayer	Man's ear cut	
Jesus betrayed	Jesus betrayed	Man healed	
Jesus arrested	Jesus arrested	Jesus arrested	
Man's ear cut	Man's ear cut		
Jesus deserted	Jesus deserted		

Order and timing of events in Gethsemane

Matthew 26:31-35 and Mark 14:27-31 say Jesus predicted Peter's denials again on the way to Gethsemane, where he prayed three times (Mark 14:32-42) and an angel attended him (Luke 22:40-46). After his first prayer, he found Peter asleep and asked why he could not stay awake for an hour (Mark 14:37). His words show this prayer lasted an hour. If he prayed the same thing a second (Mark 14:39) and third time (Matthew 26:44) each prayer lasted an hour. After each prayer he found his disciples asleep. Next Judas betrayed him. As he was arrested, Peter cut off a servant's ear with his sword, but Jesus healed him. After all his disciples deserted him, Jesus was bound and led out of the garden (Mark 14:41-5:23).

Order of events in Gethsemane

- Journey to Gethsemane (Matthew 26:30 and Mark 14:26)
- Peter's denials foretold (Matthew 26:31-35 and Mark 14:27-31)
- Jesus' first prayer (Matthew 26:36-41 and Mark 14:32-38)
- Jesus' second prayer (Matthew 26:42-43 and Mark 14:39-40)
- Jesus' third prayer (Matthew 26:44-46 and Mark 14:41-42)
- Jesus was betrayed (Mark 14:43-45 and John 18:2-9)
- Jesus was arrested (Matthew 26:50-56 and Luke 22:49-54)
- Disciples deserted Jesus (Matthew 26:56 and Mark 14:50-52)

Order of Jesus' trials and Peter's denials

The events of Jesus' trials and Peter's denials are as follows:

Matt 26:57-75	Mark 14:53-72	Luke 22:54-65	John 18:12-27
Walk to Annas	Walk to Annas	Walk to Annas	Walk to Annas
Peter followed	Peter followed	Peter followed	Peter followed
Caiaphas' trial	Caiaphas' trial	1st denial	1st denial
"I am Christ!"	"I am Christ!"	2nd denial	Annas' trial
Condemned	Condemned	3rd denial	2nd denial
1st denial	Jesus beaten	Jesus beaten	3rd denial
2nd denial	1st denial		
3rd denial	2nd denial		
	3rd denial		

Order of Jesus' trials and Peter's denials

After his arrest Jesus was taken to the high priest. It would have taken half an hour to walk there (see below). His first trial was by Annas. As he was tried, John 18:22-27 says Peter denied him the first time, and his second and third denials came after that trial. Then he was tried by Caiaphas. Matthew 26:69-75 and Mark 14:66-72 record his three denials after his trial by Caiaphas. Peter would have denied him as he was tried by both high priests. After his third denial, a rooster crowed. Jesus' own words in Mark 13:35 reveal when they crow:

"'Keep watch, because you do not know when the owner of the house will return, whether in the evening or at midnight or when the rooster crows or at dawn'" – Mark 13:35

Teaching on his return, Jesus divided night into four parts – evening; midnight; when roosters crow; and dawn. He began his division of the twelve hours of night with evening. It begins at sunset. He ended it with dawn, which is sunrise. The annual average time of sunset in Israel is 18:00 Hours and of sunrise is 06:00 Hours. The next division of night he used is midnight (24:00 Hours) – midpoint between evening and dawn. If he used the same division of time for roosters crowing then they crow at the midpoint between midnight and dawn – 03:00 Hours. According to Jesus, roosters crow at 03:00 Hours.

Timing of Peter's denials

If roosters crow at that time; Peter would have denied Jesus a third time at 03:00 Hours. His third denial came about an hour after his second (Luke 22:59-60), which would mean he denied Jesus a second time at 02:00 Hours. Luke 22:57-58 says that denial came a little after his first. How long is, 'a little after'? If fifteen minutes is a fair estimate of that time, Peter first denied Jesus at 01:45 Hours.

Timing of Jesus' trials

John 18:19 says Peter first denied Jesus at the same time as his trial by Annas began. If his first denial occurred at 01:45 Hours, that trial would have started then. John 18:25-27 says Peter's second and third denials happened after the trial by Annas ended. If his second denial came fifteen minutes after his first (Luke 22:58) and it occurred after the trial by Annas, which began at 01:45 Hours, that trial would have ended after fifteen minutes, at around 02:00 Hours.

John 18:24 says after this trial, Annas sent Jesus to be tried by Caiaphas, so that trial would have started after 02:00 Hours. After he was condemned by Caiaphas, he was put under guard (Mark 14:65). At 03:00 Hours, when Peter denied him the third time as the rooster crowed, Jesus looked at him. He recalled Jesus' words about denying him and wept (Luke 22:59-62). If it happened as Jesus was being led away by the guards, his trial by Caiaphas ended before 03:00 Hours. However, if Jesus was still being tried by Caiaphas and the Sanhedrin when he looked at Peter as he denied him the third time, this trial would have ended after 03:00 Hours. That would mean Jesus was kept under guard from around 03:00 Hours.

Order of Jesus' trials and Peter's denials

- Journey to the high priest and trial by Annas (John 18:19-24)
- Peter's first denial (Mark 14:66-68 and John 18:15-18)
- Jesus' trial by Caiaphas (Mark 14:53-65 and Luke 22:66-71)
- Jesus said, "I am Christ!" (Mark 14:61-65 and Luke 22:67-71)
- Peter's second denial (Mark 14:69-70 and John 18:25)
- Peter's third denial (Matthew 26:73-75 and Luke 22:59-62)
- Jesus was kept under guard (Mark 14:65)

Timing of other events that night

The times of Peter's denials and Jesus' trials sets events that night in the right chronology. Jesus' trial by Annas began after he arrived at his palace. If it took half an hour to walk from Gethsemane (see below) and his trial began at 01:45 Hours, the journey occurred from 01:15 to 01:45 Hours. If his betrayal and arrest took about fifteen minutes, it took place from 01:00 to 01:15 Hours.

Before his arrest, Jesus prayed three times. His first prayer lasted an hour. After he prayed, he found his disciples asleep (Mark 14:35-38). Mark 14:39 says he prayed the same thing a second time. If his first prayer lasted an hour then his second prayer lasted an hour. After that prayer he found his disciples asleep again. Matthew 26:44 says he went away and prayed the same thing again. If his first and second prayers each lasted an hour, then his third prayer also lasted an hour. It would mean Jesus prayed for three hours in Gethsemane.

Jesus woke his disciples after his third prayer then he was betrayed. If he was betrayed at 01:00 Hours, he woke them at that time. If his third prayer lasted an hour, it occurred from 24:00 Hours to 01:00 Hours. Before that prayer, he woke his disciples after he prayed the second time for an hour. He would have woken them at midnight having prayed a second time from 23:00 Hours to 24:00 Hours. That prayer began after he woke them after his first prayer. If he woke them at 23:00 Hours, his first prayed lasted from 22:00 Hours to 23:00 Hours. He prayed after arriving in Gethsemane after the Last Supper. If it took half an hour to walk there (see below), they would have left the house at 21:30 Hours. That would mean the Last Supper would have ended at 21:30 Hours having begun at 18:20 Hours.

Order and timing of other events that night

- 18:20-21:30 Hours = Last Supper (Mark 14:17-26)
- 21:30-22:00 Hours = Journey to Gethsemane (Mark 14:26-31)
- 22:00-23:00 Hours = First prayer (Mark 14:32-38)
- 23:00-24:00 Hours = Second prayer (Mark14:39-40)
- 00:00-01:00 Hours = Third prayer (Mark 14:41-42)
- 01:00-01:45 Hours = Betrayal and arrest (Mark 14:43-52)
- 01:45-03:00 Hours = Trials and denials (Mark 14:53-72)

Order of Jesus' trials by Pilate and Herod

The order of events of Jesus' trials as found in the four Gospels is:

Mt 27:1-26	Mk 15:1-15	Lk 22:66-23:25	Jn 18:28-19:16
Condemned	Condemned	Jesus is Christ	Walk to Pilate
Walk to Pilate	Walk to Pilate	Walk to Pilate	Trial by Pilate
Judas' suicide	Trial by Pilate	Trial by Pilate	"I am a king!"
Trial by Pilate	"I am a king!"	"I am a king!"	Jesus flogged
"I am a king!"	Jesus flogged	Herod's trial	Condemned
Jesus flogged	Condemned	Barabbas freed	
Condemned			

Timing of Jesus' trials by Pilate and Herod

After Jesus' trial by the Sanhedrin, he was jailed from 03:00 Hours until he was condemned at dawn (05:50 Hours[b]). If it took about ten minutes to condemn him and it took half an hour to take him to Pilate (see below), he would have arrived at his fortress after 06:30 Hours. When Judas saw Jesus had been condemned, he returned the blood money then killed himself (Matthew 27:3-10). Though Jesus said, "I am a king" during this trial, Pilate told the Jewish leaders he could find no charge against him. After learning he was from Galilee, he sent him to be tried by Herod. When he answered none of his questions, he was mocked and sent back to Pilate (Luke 23:1-12) who was performing his annual ritual of releasing a felon. He asked the crowd if they wanted him to free Jesus or Barabbas. They chose Barabbas, so Pilate released him and condemned Jesus (Mark 15:6-15). If he was crucified at 09:00 Hours (Mark 15:25) and the walk to Calvary took half an hour (see below), his trials by Pilate and Herod occurred from 06:30 Hours to 08:30 Hours.

Order of Jesus' trials by Pilate and Herod

- The religious leaders condemned Jesus to die (Mark 15:1)
- Jesus was taken to Pilate (Mark 15:1 and John 18:28)
- Judas killed himself (Matthew 27:3-10)
- Trial by Pilate (Mark 15:1-5; Luke 23:1-5 and John 18:28-32)
- Jesus said, "I am a king!" (Luke 23:3 and John 18:33-38)
- Jesus' trial by King Herod (Luke 23:7-12)
- Jesus was condemned (Mark 15:6-15 and John 19:4-16)

Order and timing of events of the Crucifixion

After Pilate condemned Jesus to die, he handed him over to his soldiers who beat and mocked him then led him out to Calvary to be crucified. Let's look at the four Gospel accounts of Jesus' crucifixion to see what they reveal about the order and timing of events:

Matt 27:31-61	Mark 15:20-47	Luke 23:26-56	John 19:17-42
Journey	Journey	Journey	Journey
Cross carried	Cross carried	Cross carried	Cross carried
Wine offered	Wine offered	Women mourn	Crucifixion
Crucifixion	Crucifixion	Crucifixion	Sign on cross
Lots cast	Lots cast	Killers forgiven	Lots cast
Sign on cross	Sign on cross	Lots cast	Jesus' mother
People mock	People mock	Rulers mock	"I thirst!"
Rulers mock	Rulers mock	Soldiers mock	Drink offered
Felons mock	Felons mock	Sign on cross	"It is finished!"
Darkness	Darkness	Felon mocks	Jesus died
Dereliction cry	Dereliction cry	Felon saved	Body on cross
Drink offered	Drink offered	Darkness	Jesus' burial
Jesus cried out	Jesus cried out	Curtain torn	
Jesus died	Jesus died	Commits spirit	
Curtain torn	Curtain torn	Jesus died	
Holy men rose	The centurion	The centurion	
The centurion	Jesus' burial	Jesus' burial	
Jesus' burial			

Order and timing of events of the Crucifixion

Pilate condemned Jesus to death and handed him over to his soldiers to prevent a riot. They flogged and mocked him then led him out to Calvary, carrying his own cross. However, when it became too much for him, the soldiers made Simon of Cyrene carry it (Mark 15:15-22). Luke 23:27-31 says on the way to Calvary Jesus turned and spoke to the women following him. He would have turned to speak to them after the cross had been taken from him. The walk to Calvary would have taken about half an hour (see below). If he was crucified at 09:00 Hours (Mark 15:25) then the journey from Pilate's Antonia Fortress would have occurred from 08:30 Hours to 09:00 Hours.

Jesus refused to drink wine mixed with myrrh to numb the pain as he was crucified between two felons. Then he asked God to forgive his killers (Luke 23:33-34). If he was nailed to the cross at 09:00 Hours (Mark 15:25), he would have asked it then. After crucifying Jesus, the four soldiers divided up his clothes by casting lots (Matthew 27:35). John 19:19-22 says when the leaders saw Pilate's sign on his cross saying; 'Jesus is the King of the Jews', they stormed off to ask him to remove it. Both events would have occurred at 09:00 Hours.

The fastest route to his fortress would have taken about twenty minutes (see below). If it took fifteen to twenty minutes to speak with Pilate and they took the same twenty-minute journey back to Calvary, this event lasted about an hour. After Jesus' clothes were divided at 09:00 Hours, he was mocked by passers-by, the Jewish leaders; the soldiers; and the two criminals being crucified with him until darkness fell from 12:00 to 15:00 Hours (Mark 15:29-33 and Luke 23:35-45). He would have been mocked on the cross from 09:00 to 12:00 Hours.

Luke 22:39-43 says when one of the criminals being crucified with Jesus mocked him, the other rebuked him then received salvation from Jesus. After Jesus' clothes were divided, he placed Mary into John's care (John 19:25-27). It seems both felons mocked him at first, but as time passed, one of them saw the man dying next to him was God's Son. This change of heart would have occurred shortly before darkness fell at 12:00 Hours. It suggests Jesus committed Mary into John's care before he gave salvation to the felon. The two events would have taken place between 09:00 Hours and 12:00 Hours.

During the time darkness fell in Israel (12:00-15:00 Hours), the Gospels record nothing. The insults ceased as Jesus suffering silently, took on all the sin and sickness of all mankind. Jesus' greatest pain was his separation from his Father. It caused him to cry out, *"My God, my God, why have you forsaken me?"* Mark 15:34-37 says Jesus said this at 15:00 Hours. Then he was offered a drink and with a loud cry he died. John 19:28-30 says after Jesus said, *"I thirst!"* he was offered a drink before he said, *"It is finished!"* then he died. Jesus would have said, *"I thirst!"* at 15:00 Hours. Luke 23:44-46 says it was 15:00 Hours when Jesus said, *"Father, into your hands I commit my spirit!"* Then he died.

The timing of Jesus' words on the cross

Jesus spoke seven times whilst he hung on the cross in agonising pain – three times after he was crucified (09:00 Hours) and before darkness fell at 12:00 Hours and four times as he died at 15:00 Hours:

09:00 Hours to 12:00 Hours

1. "Father forgive them, for they know not what they are doing."
2. "Dear woman, here is your son. Here is your mother."
3. "Today you will be with me in paradise."

15:00 Hours

4. "My God, my God, why have you forsaken me?"
5. "I thirst!"
6. "It is finished!"
7. "Into your hands I commit my spirit!"

As he died the temple curtain tore. There was an earthquake, tombs broke open and holy men came to life (Matthew 27:51-53). It made the centurion say Jesus was God (Mark 15:49). Then the crowd at the cross left (Luke 23:48). These events occurred at 15:00 Hours. The Jews did not want the bodies on the crosses when the Sabbath began at sunset. They went to ask Pilate to break the victims' legs. The fastest route to his fortress would have taken twenty minutes. It would have taken the same amount of time if they took the same route back to Calvary (see below). If it took about twenty minutes to speak with him, this event lasted about an hour, in the hour after Jesus died (15:00-16:00 Hours). At Calvary, when one of the soldiers found Jesus was dead he pierced his side with a spear (John 19:31-37).

Then Joseph of Arimathea asked Pilate for Jesus' body. If he was at the Crucifixion, it would have taken about twenty minutes to walk to Pilate's fortress and the same amount of time to return to Calvary, if he took the same route back (see below). If it took fifteen to twenty minutes to get Pilate's permission, overall, this event would have taken an hour. The sun was setting when he laid Jesus in his tomb (Luke 23:50-54) and it set that day at 18:20 Hours[b]. It was the final event of Jesus' crucifixion, as shown below:

Order of events of the Crucifixion

- Journey to Calvary (Matthew 27:31 and Mark 15:20)
- Simon carried Jesus' cross (Mark 15:21 and Luke 23:26)
- Women mourned for Jesus (Luke 23:27-31)
- Jesus was offered wine (Matthew 27:34 and Mark 15:23)
- Jesus was crucified (Matthew 27:35 and Mark 15:24-25)
- Jesus forgave his killers (Luke 23:34)
- Jesus' clothes were divided (Luke 23:34 and John 19:23-24)
- Pilate's sign on the cross (Mark 15:26 and John 19:19-22)
- Jesus and his mother Mary (John 19:25-27)
- Passers-by hurled insults (Matt 27:39-40 and Mark 15:29-30)
- The leaders mocked Jesus (Mark 15:31-32 and Luke 23:35)
- The felons mocked Jesus (Matthew 27:44 and Mark 15:32)
- The soldiers mocked Jesus (Luke 23:36-37)
- A dying felon received salvation (Luke 23:39-43)
- Darkness fell in Israel (Matthew 27:45 and Mark 15:33)
- Cry of dereliction (Matthew 27:46-49 and Mark 15:34-36)
- Jesus said, "I thirst!" (John 19:28-29)
- Jesus said, "It is finished!" (John 19:30)
- Jesus committed his spirit to his Father (Luke 23:46)
- Jesus died (Mark 15:37; Luke 23:46 and John 19:30)
- The temple curtain was torn (Mark 15:38 and Luke 23:45)
- Holy people came to life (Matthew 27:51-53)
- The centurion said Jesus was God (Mark 15:39)
- The crowd at the cross (Mark 15:40-41 and Luke 23:48-49)
- The Jews did not want bodies on the crosses (John 19:31)
- A soldier pierced Jesus' side (John 19:32-37)
- Jesus' burial (Luke 23:50-55 and John 19:38-42)

So now all of the events of Jesus' final hours have been placed in the order in which they took place. The timing of many of those events has also been established. However, it was the timing of the many journeys that took place during Jesus' final twenty-four hours that helped to cement many of the events in their correct chronology.

Journeys in Jesus' final hours

The timeframe of journeys in Jesus' final hours sets events in the right chronology. They began with his walk to Gethsemane:

Jesus' journey to Gethsemane

Christian tradition places the Upper Room near to Annas' palace. If that is correct, Jesus and his disciples would have turned right after leaving the house and headed east to the Mount of Olives. They would have passed near Annas' palace as they walked through Jerusalem's narrow streets and exited the city via the Fountain Gate before descending the slope into the Kidron Valley (John 18:1). They would have walked north along the bottom of the ravine, which separates the city on the west from the Mount of Olives on the east. At a point opposite the temple (near the present bridge), they would have turned right and climbed the slope to enter the Garden of Gethsemane, located on the lower slope of the Mount of Olives. It would have taken about half an hour to walk there[11]. If they arrived there at 22:00 Hours, they would have set out at 21:30 Hours. It would mean the Last Supper took place from 18:20 Hours to 21:30 Hours on the night before Jesus was crucified.

21:30-22:00 Hours = Jesus' journey to Gethsemane

Jesus' journey to the high priest's palace

After his arrest, Jesus would have been surrounded by guards and led out of Gethsemane, down the slope of the Mount of Olives to the path at the base of the Kidron Valley. They would have headed south along that path for about fifteen minutes then turned right and ascended the slope up to the city wall. After entering Jerusalem through the Fountain Gate, they would have travelled north along the Tyropean Valley that cut the city in two from north to south. They would have passed the Pool of Siloam then turned left before ascending the narrow streets until they reached the palace of the high priest. Christian tradition places the palace on the west hill of the city, about a hundred yards from the Upper Room. If Jesus' journey to the Mount of Olives took half an hour[12] then this journey also would have taken about half an hour[12]. If they left Gethsemane at 01:15 Hours, they would have arrived at the high priest's palace at 01:45 Hours.

01:15-01:45 Hours = Jesus' journey to the high priest's palace

Jesus' journey to Pilate's Antonia Fortress

After sentencing Jesus, the Jewish leaders took him to Pilate's Antonia Fortress to be tried by him. Guards would have led him out of Annas' palace and turned left. They would have headed north through the narrow streets to the Tyropean Valley, which split Jerusalem in two. After crossing the valley, they would have climbed the streets up the hill just north of the temple then arrived at the Western Gate of Pilate's fortress. The journey would have taken about thirty minutes[13]. If they set out after 06:00 Hours, they would have arrived at his fortress after 06:30 Hours.

06:00-06:30 Hours = Jesus' journey to Pilate's Antonia Fortress

Jesus' journeys to and from Herod's palace

When Pilate learned Jesus was a Galilean, he sent him to be tried by Herod. Soldiers would have led him out of Pilate's fortress and down to the Tyropean Valley. After crossing the valley, they would have turned west and climbed the hill to Herod's palace. It was built on the north-east shoulder of the west hill of the city and looked down on the temple area across the valley on the east. After entering the gate, Jesus would have been taken across the courtyard into the Great Hall and into Herod's presence. The walk would have taken about twenty minutes[14]. It would have occurred after Jesus' trial by Pilate began at 06:30 Hours and before he was led out to Calvary at 08:30 Hours (see below). If they took this route back to Pilate's fortress, that journey would have taken about twenty minutes[15].

06:30-08:30 Hours = Jesus' journeys to and from Herod's palace

Jesus' journey to Calvary

After being condemned, Jesus was led out to Calvary with two others carrying crosses (John 19:17-18). Each was surrounded by the soldiers who oversaw their crucifixions. Other soldiers led the way, followed by a centurion on a horse, as more soldiers brought up the rear. After exiting Pilate's fortress, they would have turned left into the narrow streets. Though crucifixions were held outside the city, the Romans liked to make a display of the victims and took them on the longest route possible through the city. They would have headed to the Tyropean Valley and after crossing it headed to the Ephraim Gate through the densely populated part of the city.

The group would have weaved its way through the crowded streets then through the Ephraim Gate, situated north of the angle where the north-west wall met the east-west wall. Beyond the gate, they would have continued along the road to Jaffa. About a hundred yards from the city gate, the centurion would have found a suitable elevated spot near the road where the crucifixions could be seen by all who passed by. It would have taken about half an hour to get there[16]. If Jesus was crucified at 09:00 Hours; this journey began at 08:30 Hours.

08:30-09:00 Hours = Jesus' journey to Calvary

The leaders' journeys to and from Pilate

When the leaders saw the sign on the cross saying Jesus was the king of the Jews, they went to ask Pilate to remove it. They would have taken the fastest route from Calvary to his fortress. They would have walked back along the road and entered Jerusalem through the Ephraim Gate. They would have navigated the bustling, narrow streets from that gate to his fortress. The journey would have taken about twenty minutes[18]. After Pilate refused their request, they would have exited his fortress, turned left and made their way through the crowded streets before exiting the city via the Ephraim Gate and on to the Crucifixion. If the walk to Calvary took about twenty minutes[19], the round trip would have taken about an hour and would have occurred in the first hour of Jesus' crucifixion.

09:00-10:00 Hours = The leaders' journeys to and from Pilate

The Jews' journeys to and from Pilate

The Jews went to ask Pilate to break the legs of the victims, so they would die and their bodies would not be on the crosses on a Sabbath. They would have taken the fastest route to his fortress from Calvary. Entering the city through the Ephraim Gate, they would have navigated the busy streets to his fortress. The journey would have taken about twenty minutes[18] soon after Jesus died at 15:00 Hours. After Pilate consented, they would have left his fortress and turned left before walking through the narrow, busy streets and exiting the city via the Ephraim Gate and walking along the road to the Crucifixion. The walk would have taken about twenty minutes[19]. The two journeys would have occurred in the hour after Jesus died.

15:00-16:00 Hours = The Jews' journeys to and from Pilate

Joseph's journeys to and from Pilate

If Joseph of Arimathea saw the Crucifixion, he would have taken the fastest route from Calvary to Pilate's fortress to ask him for Jesus' body. He would have entered the city through the Ephraim Gate and walked along the busy streets to his fortress. His journey would have taken about twenty minutes[18]. If it occurred after the Jews visited Pilate, it took place after 16:00 Hours. After Pilate consented, he would have exited his fortress and passed through the crowded streets, before exiting the city via the Ephraim Gate. Then Joseph would have walked along the road to the Crucifixion. His journey would have taken about twenty minutes[19]. It would have occurred after 16:00 Hours and before Jesus' burial at sunset (18:20 Hours).

16:00-18:20 Hours = Joseph's journeys to and from Pilate

Journeys taken in Jesus' final hours

Twelve journeys occurred in four timeframes during Jesus' final hours. The timing of these journeys helps place the events that happened in each of those four timeframes in the correct chronology.

21:30-05:50 Hours – Last Supper to condemnation

1. 30 minute-journey from the Upper Room to Gethsemane
2. 30 minute-journey from Gethsemane to Annas' palace

05:50-09:00 Hours – Condemnation to Crucifixion

3. 30 minute-journey from Annas' palace to the Antonia Fortress
4. 20 minute-journey from the Antonia Fortress to Herod's palace
5. 20 minute-journey from Herod's palace to the Antonia Fortress
6. 30 minute-journey from Pilate's Antonia Fortress to Calvary

09:00-15:00 Hours – Crucifixion to Jesus' death

7. 20 minute-journey from Calvary to Pilate to protest about sign
8. 20 minute-journey from the Antonia Fortress to Calvary

15:00-18:20 Hours – Jesus' death to his burial

9. 20 minute-journey from Calvary to Pilate to remove bodies
10. 20 minute-journey from his fortress to Calvary to kill victims
11. 20 minute-journey from Calvary to ask Pilate for Jesus' body
12. 20 minute-journey from Antonia Fortress to Calvary for burial

Final timeframe of events

The chronology of events and the journeys taken during Jesus' final hours enables them to be placed in the following timeframe:

Jesus' final hours

18:20 Hours   = Jesus arrived at the Upper Room
18:20-21:30 Hours = The Last Supper
21:30-22:00 Hours = Journey to Gethsemane
22:00-23:00 Hours = Jesus' first prayer
23:00-24:00 Hours = Jesus' second prayer
00:00-01:00 Hours = Jesus' third prayer
01:00-02:00 Hours = Betrayal, arrest, trial by Annas and Peter's denial
02:00-03:00 Hours = Trial by Caiaphas and Peter's second denial
03:00-04:00 Hours = Peter's third denial and Jesus imprisoned
04:00-05:00 Hours = Jesus imprisoned
05:00-06:00 Hours = Jesus imprisoned and condemned by leaders
06:00-07:00 Hours = Journey to Pilate's fortress and trial by him
07:00-08:00 Hours = Jesus' trials by Pilate and Herod
08:00-09:00 Hours = Jesus was condemned and taken to Calvary
09:00 Hours   = Jesus was crucified
09:00-10:00 Hours = Jesus was mocked on the cross
10:00-11:00 Hours = Jesus was mocked on the cross
11:00-12:00 Hours = Jesus was mocked and a felon was saved
12:00-13:00 Hours = Darkness came over Israel
13:00-14:00 Hours = Darkness came over Israel
14:00-15:00 Hours = Darkness in Israel as Jesus cried out
15:00 Hours   = Jesus died on the cross
15:00-16:00 Hours = Jews protested about the bodies on the crosses
16:00-17:00 Hours = Joseph asked Pilate for Jesus' dead body
17:00-18:20 Hours = Jesus' burial

Our response to Jesus' crucifixion

How do we respond to this loving God who sent His beloved Son to die for us on the cross of Calvary and receive all Jesus achieved for us through his death? We receive it by being born again (John 3:3). Being born again is something God does to us. He steps into our lives by the power of the Holy Spirit and we are born from above. He gives us His Spirit to cleanse us with holy fire and purge sin and its guilt and power in us. We come to faith in Jesus and his death on the cross. We are regenerated and made new. God gives us a new heart that is sensitive to Him and to His voice.

We are born again not physically, but spiritually. We are spiritually new – with a new nature. God puts a spiritual nature in us. We have new likes. We love God and His glory and honour and are so grateful to Him. We have new beliefs. We see Jesus as the Son of God, who is God. We see we have offended God and need Jesus, his forgiveness and his power in our lives. We see he is the everlasting Son of God and bow down and worship him. God gives us this great salvation in Jesus. When we see Jesus is the Son of God, who is God who died on the cross for our sins, we can reach out and ask him to save us and give us this abundant life by praying this prayer:

Lord Jesus Christ, I am sorry I have sinned in my life. I ask you to forgive my sin by your sacrifice on the cross. I turn from all sin. Thank you for dying for me on the cross. Come and live in my heart and be Lord of my life. Fill me with your Holy Spirit. Let this new life flow into me and through me for your glory. In Jesus' name, amen.

If you prayed this prayer, let someone in leadership know in your local church or let me know at: thejesusdiary1@gmail.com

Bibliography

[1] The Jesus Diary by John Maxwell, Amazon.com 2015
[2] Tacitus, Annals, 15.44, cited in Strobel, The Case for Christ p82 – Zondervan
[3] Suetonius – The Lives of the Caesars, Oxford World Classics
[4] Suetonius – The Lives of the Caesars, Oxford World Classics
[5] Complete Works of Josephus, Antiquities, XVIII 63f T Nelson 1998
[6] FF Bruce, Jesus and Christian Origins outside the New Testament – WB Eerdman publishing 1974
[7] F.J.A. Hort, the New Testament in the Original Greek, vol 1, p 561, Macmillan
[8] Sir F, Kenyon, The Bible and Archaeology, Harper and Row, 1940
[9] Every Day with Jesus, Selwyn Hughes, CWR, 2013
[10] Every Day with Jesus, Selwyn Hughes, CWR, 2013
[11] Ralph Gorman, CP, Last Hours of Jesus, p 40, Sheed and Ward
[12] Ralph Gorman, CP, Last Hours of Jesus, p138, Sheed and Ward
[13] Ralph Gorman, CP, Last Hours of Jesus, p141, Sheed and Ward
[14] Ralph Gorman, CP, Last Hours of Jesus, p198-9, Sheed and Ward
[15] Ralph Gorman, CP, Last Hours of Jesus, p202-3, Sheed and Ward
[16] Ralph Gorman, CP, Last Hours of Jesus, p141, Sheed and Ward
[17] Complete Works of Josephus, Antiquities, XVIII 63f T Nelson 1998
[18] Ralph Gorman, CP, Last Hours of Jesus, p202-3, Sheed and Ward
[19] Ralph Gorman, CP, Last Hours of Jesus, p202-3, Sheed and Ward

Hours[a] = Jerusalem solar calendar for sunrise and sunset times (exc. D.S.T.)

Abbreviations for names of Gospel writers

Matt or Mt = Matthew; Mk = Mark; Lk = Luke; and Jn = John

Other titles by John Maxwell

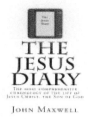

THE JESUS
JESUS
DIARY
THE MOST COMPREHENSIVE
CHRONOLOGY OF THE LIFE OF
JESUS CHRIST, THE SON OF GOD

JOHN MAXWELL

THE JESUS DIARY

THE CHRONOLOGY OF JESUS' LIFE – PART 1

'The Jesus Diary' is the most comprehensive chronology of events in the life of Jesus the Son of God ever written.

Jesus visited Earth at a point in history. The Gospels give four accounts of the one story of his birth, life, death and resurrection. '*The Jesus Diary*' is Part 1 of 'The Chronology of Jesus' Life' series. It puts the events of his life in the order they occurred and when they happened in history. The result is the most detailed timeframe of events in his life ever written. This helps solidify the faith of all who believe and satisfies the curiosity of those who seek to know if and when God walked on Earth. It is a great study aid for pastors, preachers, and Bible students, as it reveals:

- The year Jesus was born and how long he spent in Egypt
- When Jesus was baptised and his ministry began
- When John the Baptist was executed and Jesus fed the 5,000
- The exact date Jesus was transfigured
- The hour, the day and the year that Jesus died
- The dates Jesus rose again and ascended into heaven

40 DAYS OF RESURRECTION APPEARANCES
THE CHRONOLOGY OF JESUS' LIFE – PART 3

For the first time, Jesus' forty days of resurrection appearances are broken down into forty, day-by-day sections, which reveal:

- The number and order of Jesus' resurrection appearances
- How many people risen Jesus appeared to
- The significance of the locations where Jesus appeared
- The day and date Jesus, the Son of God rose from the dead
- The dates of Jesus' appearances in Jerusalem and Galilee
- The day and date risen Jesus ascended into heaven

'*40 Days of Resurrection Appearances*' is Part 3 of 'The Chronology of Jesus' Life' series. It takes an in-depth, day-by-day look at how Jesus' appearances break down into a forty-day period. It reveals when he appeared to his disciples and when he did not. There is as much to learn about him and his disciples from the times when he did not appear to them as there is when he did appear to them. Join me on this day-by-day journey of forty days to find what they learned from Jesus' appearances and absences and how their experiences can be applied to our lives today. It will change the way we view Jesus and his resurrection and the way we view ourselves.

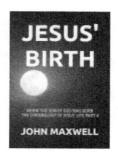

JESUS' BIRTH

THE CHRONOLOGY OF JESUS' LIFE – PART 4

A forensic examination of the information recorded in the Gospels regarding Jesus' birth to establish when he was born.

'Jesus' Birth' is Part 4 of 'The Chronology of Jesus' Life' series. It establishes when he was born and sets the existence of God's Son on Earth in history using Roman and Jewish historical records. Also, this book examines the 'missing years' between his birth and his baptism and what it means to us today. In this book you will discover:

- The exact year in which Jesus was born
- The age difference between Jesus and John the Baptist
- How long baby Jesus spent in Egypt
- When Jesus visited the temple in Jerusalem as a child
- What Jesus did in the years between his birth and his baptism
- When Jesus' public ministry began

There is historical information in the Gospels for when Jesus was born and when he was baptised and his ministry began. The writer has taken that information and combined it with great numeracy skills to establish the year Jesus, the Son of God was born in human form on Earth. Enjoy this informative and revealing read as it transforms your opinions about Jesus' birth, his existence and his deity.

HISTORICAL JESUS

'*Historical Jesus*' is the most comprehensive chronology of events in the ministry of Jesus, the Son of God ever written.

Jesus, God's Son visited this Earth at a point in history. The Gospels give four accounts of the one story of Jesus' ministry. '*Historical Jesus*' sets all of the events of Jesus' ministry in the order they occurred and places each one on a specific date in history. From this most detailed chronology of events, the writer explores all the aspects of his ministry from a chronological perspective, which give great insights into Jesus' miracles, teachings, prayers, healings and the prophecies made about him. Also, it examines the main characters in Jesus' time of ministry and his relationships with those people.

Great tool for pastors, preachers and students

'*Historical Jesus*' will help preachers eliminate chronological inaccuracies from their sermons, which will increase the impact of their message. The book is a great study aid for Bible students as it reveals:

- The year Jesus was born and how long he spent in Egypt
- When Jesus was baptised and his Galilean ministry began
- When John the Baptist was killed and Jesus fed the 5,000
- The hour-by-hour breakdown of Jesus' final hours
- The exact times that Peter denied Jesus
- The dates Jesus died, rose again and ascended into heaven

An ideal gift for Church leaders

'*Historical Jesus*' is the ideal gift for pastors, leaders, preachers and lovers of the Bible as it contains a wealth of material useful for sermons and teaching. It will be a real blessing to all who receive it.

40 DAYS – JESUS' TEMPLATE FOR HIS CHURCH
HOW HE WANTS HIS CHURCH TO OPERATE

After Jesus rose from the dead, he appeared to his disciples over a period of forty days. At each appearance, he revealed different aspects of how he wanted his Church to operate.

This book shows that at each resurrection appearance, Jesus revealed to the disciples the elements that were to be included each time his Church met. On the days he did not appear, all the teachings, healings and miracles from his ministry are viewed through his disciples' eyes after they saw his death and resurrection. It gives wonderful insights into their character and personalities.

This book reveals Jesus intended his Church to be based on the words he spoke and all that is written about him in the Scriptures. It was to be a place of love, joy, peace, healing, restoration, giving, praise and prayer. It was to be a place where sermons reveal him in the Scriptures and where miracles, signs, wonders, testimonies, prophecies and Holy Communion occurred each time his people met. The meeting was to be so full of life and joy and revelation that those who were present could not wait to share with others what they had learned about Jesus. This book shows his Church was to be a place where all are welcome to come to seek him and voice their doubts – a place where those doubts would be listened to by loving and caring leaders who would turn them to faith.

In many parts of the world today, the Church is not operating as Jesus intended. Christian leaders and all who run churches need to return to Jesus' mandate for his Church. This book shows how Jesus intended his Church to operate. When we operate our churches in the way Jesus intended, they will be filled with people full of the joy of the Lord and the fullness of life Jesus came to bring them. Also the Church will have the full impact on the world that he intended.

JESUS HEALS

Throughout his ministry Jesus preached the Good News of the kingdom of God, healed the sick and cast out demons. He did so many miracles the world would not have enough room for the books that would be written (John 21:25). Yet only thirty-six are recorded in the Gospels. As all Scripture is God-breathed, it means the Holy Spirit, through the Gospel writers recorded them for a specific purpose. 'Jesus Heals' examines the thirty-six miracles to see what those purposes are and what they reveal about Jesus and his miracles and healings and how they apply to us today. In this book you will discover:

- The different ways in which people came to Jesus for healing
- The different ways in which people received their healing
- Jesus not only heals, but restores us in all ways
- Jesus has the power and authority to heal
- Jesus is willing and able to heal all who come to him
- How to receive healing from Jesus

The miracles are examined in thirty-six chapters. Each miracle reveals different aspects of God's kingdom and the variety of ways Jesus performed his healings and miraculous signs. It shows the levels of faith and the different ways people came to Jesus for healing, which inspires us to approach Jesus in faith for our healing today. Faith comes by hearing and hearing by the Word of God. As we read the Word of God, as we hear it and take it into our hearts, our souls and our bodies, it is Spirit and it is Life to us.

A helpful tool for pastors and preachers

For pastors and preachers, each chapter in the book can be used as a sermon. Some miracles and healings can be put together for one talk or for a series of talks. The final part of the book summarises the miracles, but after looking at the miracles, you may form your own conclusions. I pray that as you read this book that like me, you will be healed even before you finish reading it. If not, then keep on reading until you are healed. All Glory to God!

MY STORY, HIS GLORY

'My story, His Glory' is the testimony of the conversion of John Maxwell. In August 1994, John, who was not a Christian, went to St. Andrew's Church in Hong Kong. He sat in a pew, disliking every minute of the experience and vowing never to go again when suddenly he felt a fire flowing up and down his body. All his angst left him and a wonderful peace filled him. At the end of the service the first thing he said was, "I can't wait for next week." He entered the church vowing to never go again and left it eagerly looking ahead to the next service. That eagerness has never left him.

However, that was just the start of a set of extraordinary events that saw John prophesy a week later. Then he had dreams where he was taken up to heaven where he heard God both speak and laugh. After that, he had wonderful, supernatural encounters that could only have been orchestrated by God. He received wonderful words of knowledge to help others receive breakthroughs in their lives. The baptism of fire John received that day in St. Andrew's Church in Hong Kong during the movement of the Holy Spirit in the time of the Toronto Blessing is real and available to people today.

If you hunger for that fire, join John as he looks at the supernatural events that took place around his conversion. It is journey that will encourage and inspire you to receive the baptism of the Holy Spirit.

The ideal gift for those seeking salvation

'My Story, His Glory' is a great gift to give to anyone searching for God and eternal life or to a loved one with whom you want to share the good news about Jesus. It is the perfect reading companion for anyone doing the Alpha Course or other basic Christianity course.

All available in paperback or hardback at Amazon.com or Amazon.co.uk

Printed in Great Britain
by Amazon

23935553R00099